'David Lawson's voice is tender, his vision lucid and compassionate and his embrace universal. He has the unique capacity of instructing by example. A rare gift.'

KITTY CAMPION, AUTHOR OF *A Woman's Herbal*

'Working with David has been a truly enlightening experience for me!'

DR BARBARA A. KING, HOLISTIC MEDICAL PRACTITIONER

'David Lawson takes you on a healing journey that everyone can benefit from.'

LOUISE L. HAY, AUTHOR OF *You Can Heal Your Life*

THORSONS

PRINCIPLES

OF

SELF-HEALING

DAVID LAWSON

Thorsons

An Imprint of HarperCollins*Publishers*

Thorsons
An Imprint of HarperCollins*Publishers*
77–85 Fulham Palace Road
Hammersmith, London W6 8JB
1160 Battery Street
San Francisco, California 94111–1213
Published by Thorsons 1996

10 9 8 7 6 5 4 3 2 1

A catalogue record for this book
is available from the British Library

ISBN 1 85538 486 8

Text illustrations by Tony Hannaford

Printed in Great Britain by
HarperCollinsManufacturing Glasgow

THIS BOOK IS DEDICATED TO MY PARENTS
LILIAN AND ERIC, WHOSE CARE AND SUPPORT
HAVE ALWAYS BEEN THERE FOR ME.
WITH LOVE, DAVID

ABOUT THE AUTHOR:

David Lawson is an English healer, writer and course leader. Together with his partner Justin Carson he travels the world teaching self-healing techniques, hands-on healing, psychic development and spiritual growth.

Sometimes he just stops to enjoy the view.

His books include *Star Healing: Your Sun Sign, your Health and your Success* (Hodder & Stoughton), *Money and your Life: A Prosperity Playbook* (with Justin Carson; Healing Workshops Press) and, for Thorsons, *I See Myself in Perfect Health: Your Essential Guide to Self-Healing* and the forthcoming title *Principles of Psychic Potential*.

His audio tapes include the guided visualizations *I See Myself in Perfect Health* volumes I and II and the *Money and your Life Prosperity Course*, all produced by Healing Workshops Press.

David and Justin are authorized world-wide facilitators of courses based on *You Can Heal Your Life* by Louise L. Hay. For details of these and other forthcoming events based upon their own self-healing material please write to:

Healing Workshops
PO Box 1678
London NW5 4EW
UK

CONTENTS

ACKNOWLEDGEMENTS

I would like to thank the following people for their help in the writing and publication of this book:

Susan Mears (my agent), Elizabeth Puttick (my commissioning editor), Michelle Pilley, Michele Turney, Barbara Vesey, Elizabeth Hutchins, Jo Ridgeway, Michael Spender, Tony Hannaford, Barbara A. King, Lilian and Eric Lawson, Anne and Alex Carson, Star, Stephanie Holland, The Delicious Kitty Campion and all of my friends, family, clients and guides.

Special thanks to Louise L. Hay for her inspiration and encouragement, and also to my partner Justin Carson whose practical support, ideas, good humour and care make it possible for me to write.

DAVID LAWSON
LONDON, JANUARY 1996

Please note that to protect the confidentiality of the friends and clients who have kindly contributed their stories to this book I have altered names and details accordingly.

The publishers would like to thank Jillie Collings for her suggestion for the title of this series, *Principles of...*

A PERSONAL NOTE

BY JUSTIN CARSON

'Healing' is not something that can be 'done' to us, it requires our active participation in changing our thoughts, changing our old emotional patterns and ultimately changing our circumstances so that we can engender a healthier state of being.

This is an exceptional book in the field of 'self-healing' in that it doesn't eschew tried and tested medical techniques. We are, however, asked to learn how to balance the advice and knowledge of medical and complementary practitioners with our own innate healing skills. In doing so we can change the patterns in our lives that have helped to create our problems and ailments in the first place.

Reading this book will furnish you with all the tools that you need to start changing the ingrained mental and emotional patterns that you have learned from early childhood. Applying these techniques will help you emerge as a healthier and more empowered person.

'Healing' is also about quality of life. Not everyone will get well again, but we can all learn to live with honour, dignity and courage, whatever the future holds. While self-healing is primarily concerned with extending and celebrating life, for some, the process of dying can produce the greatest healing of all.

David Lawson is a warm and skilful healer; everyone who comes into contact with him departs recharged and invigorated by his kindness, skill and words of wisdom.

I trust that you will enjoy this book as much as I have and that it will benefit you in countless, and as yet unimaginable, ways.

JUSTIN CARSON
HEALER AND COURSE LEADER

BEGINNING THE JOURNEY

THE ADVENTURE OF HEALING

Self-healing is an ongoing adventure, a voyage of self-discovery where each of us has the opportunity to explore a multitude of choices and solutions to our ever-changing needs. Whether we begin our journey completely healthy or in the midst of dealing with a physical illness, mental problem or emotional need, there is much to discover and to put into practice that will enhance our lives in ways that go beyond our wildest dreams. Our ticket as we embark upon this adventure is a desire to learn and grow, our passport a willingness to change our lives for the better.

Your desire may already be clear to you. Perhaps you wish to stay healthy and prevent the onset of illness, disease or disharmony. Perhaps you are looking for support in dealing with an existing health problem and making the most of the medical or complementary therapies that you are encountering along the way.

For some of you reading this book, your need or desire may be less specific. Perhaps you wish to exorcise some ghosts from your past or create a greater sense of wholeness, inner peace, confidence, self-esteem and forward direction. In some cases

you may wish to build on the foundation of well-being and happiness that you already have in your life, to discover more joy, more freedom and greater opportunities for fulfilment.

This book explores the *principles of* self-healing; these principles can be adapted to help you with any aspect of life-enhancement or personal development. The principles that underpin any exercise that focuses on physical healing can equally be directed to helping with emotional, mental or spiritual needs. Please use the ideas and techniques that are appropriate for you and be creative in adapting them for your own special requirements.

WHAT IS SELF-HEALING?

Self-healing is a continual process of taking charge of your health, well-being and personal potential. It comes from actively seeking solutions to the many challenges that we face in our lives rather than seeing ourselves as victims of fate. Instead of doing our best to negotiate a route through the ups and downs of our existence we can make a decision to create the life that we desire and to live it to the best of our ability.

- Self-healing is using the powers of your mind positively and constructively. To heal and develop your life, you need to be willing to discard the old thoughts, beliefs and attitudes that no longer support you in health and harmony, and exchange them for new ones that do.

- Self-healing is listening to the intelligence and wisdom of your body. You need to be aware of your physical needs and you need to take action to exercise, feed and think about your body in ways that are loving and healthy.

- Self-healing is harnessing the creative, positive energy of your emotions. You need to be willing to listen to your heart, acknowledge your feelings and express them safely and effectively.

- Self-healing is also about finding your place in the greater scheme of things and developing a philosophy or a spiritual awareness that gives your life a sense of meaning. You need to be willing to expand your view of the world and entertain the joyful mysteries of the universe, regardless of your background, culture or the beliefs that you were brought up with.

This book is a guide to the powers of your mind and your ability to make new choices that will allow mental, emotional, physical and spiritual changes to occur in your life. It is for you to decide to act upon those choices, but each little step forward, no matter how small, can be a giant leap towards self-healing and personal development.

HOW CAN WE STAY HEALTHY?

Very simply, we stay healthy when we remain in balance. It helps to be in balance with other people and with our environment, but the most important place to start is with ourselves. To be in harmony with the world around us it is often best to begin by creating harmony within and then work outwards. To have our lives in balance we need to balance ourselves physically, mentally, emotionally and spiritually.

Finding balance is not about sticking to a rigid formula. It is not a case of learning how to do all the right things and holding it there. For example, if you were shown how to place your body in perfect physical alignment so that your posture was 100 per cent correct, you would have been done a great service. If, however, you were encouraged to hold yourself rigidly in one correct position so that you would never lose that perfect alignment, you would have been done a great disservice. Life is about constant change and movement; being balanced is never going to look quite the same twice.

As we progress through the ideas and techniques that I am sharing here with you I will be encouraging you to remember and use the four key principles of self-healing: to listen, to notice, to choose and to adapt.

LISTENING

Some of us are born with good listening skills; some of us learn them from our parents or parent figures; some of us learn by necessity later on in life. Are you a good listener? However good you are there is always something new that you can learn about listening.

Listening is not dependent on our ability to hear. People with impaired hearing can sometimes be better at listening than people whose hearing is clear and perfect.

To heal ourselves we need to listen to our feelings, listen to our bodies, listen to the words that we use, listen to the sound of or feel the vibration of our voices, listen to the information that is coming to us from other people and from our environment. When we listen, we are blessed with all the information that we need to make wonderful healing changes in our lives.

NOTICING

When we notice something it often takes on a power or a significance that it did not previously have. When we notice a beautiful flower, a wonderful fragrance or a captivating sound our mood may change; thoughts, memories or associations may come to mind that were not present before. Similarly, if we notice something unpleasant then it may also take on a significance for us and affect our mood – but by noticing it we can make a choice to change it or, alternatively, to change our response to it.

To heal ourselves we need to be willing to notice our thoughts and beliefs, notice what motivates us and gives us energy, notice what de-motivates us and depletes our energy. It helps to notice the images, inspirations and insights that we receive. Noticing gives us power and helps us to take positive action.

CHOOSING

So many of us put up with the unsatisfactory or unhealthy elements of our lives because we do not realize that we have the power of choice. We tend to believe that life is something that happens to us regardless of our wishes, dreams or desires, and we often picture ourselves as victims of circumstance doing our best to cope with the hand that we have been dealt.

When we learn that we have a choice and that we have a right to exercise that choice in all areas of our health and

happiness, we discover that we have the power to make wonderful changes.

To heal ourselves we often need to choose new ways of thinking and acting. This includes choosing new ways to look at life, choosing to let go of anything that no longer supports our health and happiness and choosing new directions that will enhance our personal development. When we exercise our choice we create new options for ourselves and we take charge of our destiny.

ADAPTING

Some illnesses and many problems are created as a direct result of our basic fear of and resistance to life. Even the most positive, go-ahead people may fear or resist some areas of change. In contrast, some of the healthiest people I have met have been those with a great willingness to adapt and learn new ways of approaching life.

To heal ourselves we often need to adapt to changing circumstances: adapting to different environments, adapting to changing needs and desires, adapting our approach to obtain the best results in all situations, adapting ideas, techniques, treatments and philosophies. When we are willing to adapt we remain flexible and open to solutions that go beyond our previous expectations or experience.

When we continue to listen, notice, choose and adapt then we are able to create and re-create balance within ourselves, allowing our passage through life to be as healthy and happy as it was always meant to be. This is particularly important when we need to respond to the message of illness.

While it is always preferable to stay balanced and prevent illness from occurring as much as possible, the advent of illness can be a gift, especially when we choose to look at our situation positively and with love. It is true that we may not feel that our illness is a blessing when it is painful or uncomfortable and when it inhibits us from living life to the full, but we still have it within our power to turn it into a beneficial gift rather than a curse.

Illness always brings a message. Physical symptoms tell us that there is something we need to learn about ourselves and something we need to change. The message may be a predominantly physical one. If we have a backache then the message might be that we need to learn to move in a different way or that we need to learn to stand correctly. Listening to your body and noticing aches and pains early on can allow you to choose new ways of correcting them by finding out about, for example, appropriate exercise, therapies and postural training. Even if you begin to take heed of the aches after some damage has already occurred, there is much you can do to improve the situation and prevent further deterioration.

With physical symptoms, however, the message may also be emotional. The backache that requires us to move, lift and stand in a healthier way can also require us to look at the cause of the emotional tension that is contributing to the pain or discomfort we are experiencing.

Alternatively, the message may be a mental one: perhaps we are viewing ourselves and our lives in ways that rigidly adhere to old patterns of belief that no longer suit us. Rigid thinking is one cause of rigidity within the body; the pain may be telling us that we need to change the way that we view our current situation.

Physical symptoms all tell us that there is something that we need to know and, in many cases, something that we need to do to heal our lives. It is similar with emotional problems, accidents, break-downs of communication, challenging relationships and periods of crisis or disturbance. Everything contains a message and everything is a gift if we remain open and willing to use it as one.

THE HEAD, THE HEART AND THE VOICE

Many natural healing traditions work by aligning the head, the heart and the voice. Native American and other indigenous cultures from around the world have systems of healing that are passed down from generation to generation. They include the use of natural medicines, sacred rituals and an understanding of human nature that so-called civilized cultures are having to relearn. An essential understanding of human nature includes the knowledge that when the head, the heart and the voice are in conflict then there will be an imbalance, and disease or disharmony will follow.

The head is, of course, our unique collection of thoughts, beliefs attitudes, judgements and opinions; the heart is our wealth of feelings, emotions, instincts and physical sensations; the voice is our expression, our communication and our creativity. The modern world places a strong emphasis on the head. We live at a time when the pace is generally getting faster and the technology that we are using makes it necessary for us to update and expand our knowledge constantly. Our educational systems are more concerned with the acquisition of facts than they are with teaching us to express ourselves properly and to be in touch with our feelings and intuition.

It is true that the numerous advances in technology, science and human knowledge are miraculous gifts. If used with wis-

dom and awareness they can transform many areas of our lives
for the better – but we need to keep ourselves balanced in order
to develop that wisdom. For each of us individually, keeping
our heads, hearts and voices in alignment is the best way that
we can negotiate and transcend the stresses of modern living.

SUZANNE'S STORY

Suzanne was a woman with a very passionate, expressive nature
whose instincts compelled her to respond to life with emotion, compassion and sensitivity. When she first came to me for a healing and
counselling session she was feeling stuck and frustrated. Nothing
seemed to be working for her in her career or personal life and she
had regular periods of depression. Sometimes her depressions would
last for weeks; she described them as being marooned from life as if
she were living on some colourless desert island, disconnected from
the rest of the world.

Experiences like this can be very common. Many of us have felt cut
off from other people or cut off from ourselves. Listening to this sensitive person talk about her life I became aware that I could hear different messages coming from different parts of her being. I shared
the idea with Suzanne that we all need to have our heads, our hearts
and our voices in alignment, and asked her to tell me what she was
feeling in her heart.

Suzanne told me how she was often easily moved to tears – anything from a beautiful piece of music to the simplest gesture of love
would bring tears of joy, sadness and release. She also told me that
during her periods of depression she sometimes lost her ability to feel
anything and that would distress her. At times she would have the
pain of emotion sticking in her throat. Indeed, she regularly suffered
from a sore throat and occasionally lost her voice completely.

I asked her what she thought about her emotions and Suzanne
told me that she loved to have them but that she was afraid that they
might be a bad thing. She thought that it was not healthy to be too

emotional. When she was a little girl Suzanne's father had told her off for being 'too sensitive'. He had told her that she ought to control her emotions because to do otherwise left her open to being taken advantage of by other people. He had given her the idea that to be strong and self-reliant meant hiding her sensitivity away from the world.

Suzanne's heart was filled with positive, emotional energy but her head was filled with many limiting beliefs and judgements about expressing her emotion. The result was that Suzanne's voice was confused: sometimes it expressed the feelings that were present and sometimes it choked them back, literally, and that was when Suzanne became sick or depressed. The colour and inspiration of Suzanne's life were all tied up in her emotional nature, and it was through her feelings that she had the most valuable contact with other people and with the world around her. It is no surprise that she felt marooned on a colourless island when she felt restrained from expressing herself.

The more that Suzanne let go of her judgements and allowed herself to be sensitive and passionate, the more joyful she felt, the less depressed she was and the more her life worked for her. She learned to think and speak in ways that expressed her true nature, and her head, her heart and her voice moved into alignment. It is interesting to note that when she gave herself full permission to be emotional she discovered that she did not always need to be. What is more, she learned to feel strong and safe whether she was emotional or not.

THOUGHTS, FEELINGS AND EXPRESSION

For many of us the conflict between the feelings or desires of our hearts and the beliefs and judgements that we hold in our heads can create stress in our bodies that manifests as physical illness or repetitive problems whether in our relationships, our careers or our financial security. Our voices are left confused, expressing mixed messages or, in some cases, very little at all. We do not say what we mean, nor do we truly mean what we say.

If, for example, we feel very angry because someone we love has abused or disregarded us in some way but we hold a belief that we do not have the right to be angry, we may find ourselves expressing anger in indirect ways such as by whining, moaning, being sarcastic or blaming ourselves for our predicament. Sooner or later that tension will create an illness inside us or adversely affect our ability to communicate properly with other people.

The good news is that we always have a choice to change this kind of damaging pattern, trading in unhealthy beliefs for healthy ones and releasing destructive forms of communication in favour of the kind of expression that will bring us positive results. In this way we can always help ourselves to stay in good health.

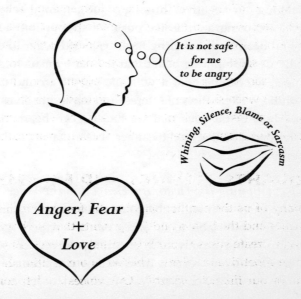

By changing our negative, limiting or judgemental beliefs into positive, accepting, permissive ones we support our feelings, needs and desires, discovering healthy, loving ways to express them. By developing the belief that it is safe for us to express our anger, we can be honest with the people around us, seek new solutions to conflicts of interest and leave ourselves free to express more of the love that we have in our hearts. Love is often trapped and obscured by anger or fear that we feel unable to express and let go of.

Exercise: Aligning the Head, the Heart and the Voice

For this exercise you will need 20 minutes of peace and quiet, somewhere comfortable to sit, and a pen and paper.

Start by sitting quietly and breathing deeply, consciously slowing down your breath a little so that you become settled and calm.

Next, think about one specific health issue that you have, or something else that is challenging you at the moment. It could be a problem with a relationship or some aspect of your work that is frustrating you.

Focus first on your heart. Take a few moments to ask yourself the question *'What do I feel about this in my heart?'* If it helps, you could place your hand on your chest and imagine that, as you breathe, you breathe directly into your heart and the feelings that you have inside you.

Do you feel sad?

Do you feel angry?

Do you feel joyful? confused? numb? disappointed? hurt? passionate? excited? scared?

Do you have desires or needs pulsing away in your heart that need to be acknowledged and expressed?

Listen to your feelings and notice them.

Next, focus on your head. Ask yourself the question *'What do I think about this?'* As you breathe, imagine that you are able to shine a light on to your thoughts and beliefs to make them more visible. Ask yourself:

'What do I think about this health issue, challenge or problem?'

'What do I think about my feelings?'

'Is it safe for me to feel like this?'

'Do I have judgements about my feelings?

'Do I have negative or limiting thoughts about this situation?'

Listen to your thoughts and beliefs and notice them.

Take a few moments to write down what you feel and think.

Now focus on your voice. Placing a hand gently on your throat, ask yourself *'What do I need to say about this?'* As you breathe, imagine your throat relaxing and ask yourself:

'Do I need to express my feelings?'

'Do I need to ask for help?'

'Do I need to communicate my desires or requirements?'

'Do I need to ask for information?'

'Could I be more honest with myself or someone close to me?'

Again, write down any thoughts or feelings that you have.

What new choices can you make to deal with your health issue or your situation in a different way?

How can you adapt your thoughts, beliefs and actions to help you to heal this challenge?

Make a note of any insights that you receive, and remember to act upon them. Repeat this exercise regularly. The more that you ask yourself the right questions, the easier it becomes for you to connect your heart, head and voice and the easier it is for you to take positive action.

As we progress through this book I will be sharing many ideas and techniques for developing positive, healthy patterns of thought, expressing and using the power of your feelings and maintaining your life in harmony and balance. This is just the beginning.

Visualization: Harmonizing your Thoughts, Feelings and Expression

Find somewhere quiet and comfortable to sit, unplug the telephone and make sure that you are not going to be disturbed. Sit with your back supported and your body open and relaxed, your arms and legs uncrossed. If you prefer you can lie down, but again make sure that you keep your

PRINCIPLES OF SELF-HEALING

I am about to invite you to use some positive mental images. This is a little like having a daydream or consciously picturing something that you desire or something that you wish to remember. Some people have strong images when they do this, some do not. It is enough to hold the idea or concept in your mind for this exercise to work for you.

To begin, breathe deeply and imagine your heart and your chest pulsing with a beautiful healing light. The light is a shimmering mass of iridescent colours that reflect your current mood and feelings. Choose the strongest colours and see them glowing brighter and brighter at your heart.

Next, imagine your throat, your neck and your voice box also glowing with light; notice the strongest colours that fill and surround this area of your body. See the light becoming stronger, healthier and more positive.

Then, concentrate on your head and your mind and imagine this area also glowing with light. What colours would be glowing from your mind? See light shimmering around your head as you explore and play with your many passing thoughts.

Finally, see a single, pure beam of golden light connecting your head, your heart and your voice, a strong line of light energy that joins up the emotional area of your chest to the area of communication in your throat and the area of thought located within your head.

Imagine the coloured light in all three areas harmonizing and growing brighter still as your head, your heart and your voice come into instant alignment and balance. Imagine yourself thinking, feeling and communicating with one strong positive voice; all parts of yourself are in balance and in agreement with each other. Continue to breathe deeply and hold this image or concept for a while, noticing your thoughts, feelings, needs and desires.

Repeat this exercise again when you need to regain some balance or when you wish to heal some internal or external conflict. In the meantime, let us continue by healing some of the thoughts and beliefs that you may be holding in your mind...

HEALING YOUR MIND

THE REALMS OF BRILLIANCE AND CONFLICT

Your mind is extraordinary. Nobody else thinks in exactly the same way as you do. No one has quite the same collection of thoughts, beliefs, memories, dreams and ideas that you have. You are special!

Much of the time our minds serve us extremely well. For most of us, the way that we think keeps us alive and helps us to function quite effectively. However, there may be areas of disharmony, conflict and ill health that are caused in part by the limiting, restrictive or judgemental beliefs that we hold. We can even think our way into illness and crisis without being aware of what we are doing.

The mind is very busy; it likes to create constant activity and it likes to stay in control of what is going on. This busy-ness and the need to control can create stress and rigidity. We need to learn to harness the power of our minds and use it constructively so that we can create the space to grow in health and happiness.

NEGATIVE AND LIMITING BELIEFS

Even the most positive people have areas of thought or belief that do not support their health and well-being. This does not mean that they are actively doing something wrong, just that – like everyone else on the planet – they need to grow beyond some of the ways they have learned to think.

As children, we rapidly absorb information about the world around us. We listen to our parents, our guardians, our brothers and sisters, our teachers and our playmates and pick up a wealth of ideas and information about ourselves, other people and the nature of the world that we live in. Some of this information is healthy, some of it is not.

On the whole, the beliefs that we learn work very well for us. Even if they are negative or limiting they often keep us safe and help us to survive during the more vulnerable periods of our lives. Chiefly we learn the best ways to gain the approval or attention of anyone who is there to look after us. Our patterns of behaviour, our thoughts and our beliefs reflect this.

As we grow up, we naturally review this knowledge, changing many of our ideas and beliefs along the way. This is part of learning and growing; we are listening to information, noticing the behaviour of the people around us, choosing our ideas and adapting to the situations we find ourselves in. The tension comes when we remain unaware of beliefs that are unhealthy for us or when we get a bit stuck in patterns of thought and behaviour that may once have been valid but now no longer reflect our needs, desires and aspirations.

SAM'S STORY

Sam was a man in his mid-thirties who came to me complaining of minor aches and pains. He constantly sought relief for his discomfort but had lost faith in the treatments he had previously attempted. He often did not complete them and his life was a catalogue of failures. He had lived through a series of unfulfilling relationships, dissatisfying jobs and missed opportunities.

We did some guided relaxation work together. I used positive thoughts and soothing visual images to settle Sam into a relaxed state and help him to release some of the tension that was contributing to his aches and pains. As he settled, Sam began to talk about his childhood and I began to hear some of his deeply held negative and limiting beliefs.

When Sam was a small child his parents had separated and Sam's mother was left to bring up four children on her own. Money was scarce and Sam's mother was so busy providing for her children that she rarely had the time or energy left over to give them all the attention they needed. Like most children, Sam would ask for toys and sweets, and would do his best to get a little extra attention. His mother would respond by telling him honestly that she did not have the time or did not have the money to give him what he wanted.

When she became over-tired or fed up with the constant demands Sam's mother would say, *'Stop asking! You can't have what you want so there's no point in continuing to ask. You just can't have what you want!'* By the age of seven, Sam stopped asking. He became quite withdrawn and started to get minor illnesses, nurturing his little hurts, aches and pains. He did not complain very much because he had learned that there was no point in asking for things; at the same time his withdrawal earned him some approval from his mother, who felt less pressured by her least demanding child. He developed a belief that his needs could not be met.

As Sam grew up he automatically changed some of his beliefs. He found that he could earn money for himself and that there was not always a shortage of resources. However, he still held a basic belief that his needs would never be met and that it was not all right to ask for what he wanted. He also held a belief that there was not enough attention to go around, so he always formed relationships with

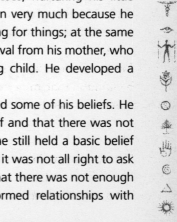

women who were never quite available when he needed them. He often found himself surrounded by friends and colleagues who were distant and unavailable, too.

The more he relaxed, the more Sam was able to talk about his past and the more he too saw the connections between his childhood experiences, his deeply held beliefs and the patterns that he was living out in his adult life. Sam realized that his aches and pains came from the frustration of his unexpressed needs and the guilt that he felt about having those needs in the first place.

Together we created some positive thoughts for Sam to use regularly so that he could re-train himself to be available for more fulfilling experiences. These positive thoughts included:

- IT IS SAFE AND EASY FOR ME TO HAVE MY NEEDS MET.

- MY LIFE IS RICH AND FULFILLING.

and

- IT IS SAFE FOR ME TO ASK FOR WHAT I WANT.

By talking about his experiences and using positive thoughts to create some new, healthier beliefs, Sam was able to make some wonderful changes. His aches and pains soon dissolved and his life became richer, more satisfying and more nourishing.

THOUGHTS ARE ENERGY

Have you ever eaten something that has disagreed with you? Some foods do not suit us very well, they sit uncomfortably on the stomach, they are depleting and they may trigger an allergic reaction or lower our energy levels. If you eat a lot of foods like this your body may adjust so that you are less aware of their impact, but they are still depleting you, lowering your immune system and perhaps even causing long-term health problems. The same can be true for negative or limiting thoughts.

Our thoughts are energy. Every thought that we have contains its own unique quality and substance. We can imagine this energy as a subtle electrical charge that radiates into every cell of our bodies and creates a field of influence that surrounds us. What is more, the energy of our thoughts has its own magnetism which attracts similar or complementary energy to it. What this means is that our thoughts strongly contribute to the experiences that we create in our lives. It is said that we are what we eat. Perhaps it could also be said that we are what we think.

When we think a positive thought, we fill and surround ourselves with the positive energy of that thought. Positive energy boosts the immune system, maintains us in balance and makes us available for positive experiences, positive people, positive opportunities and healthy solutions. Similarly, negative thoughts send out a negative energy that affects our health, our balance and our experiences, but the impact is quite different. Just like unsuitable foods, negative thoughts are depleting and disempowering. In some cases they can even give us a form of mental, emotional and physical indigestion.

We have free choice. When we listen to our thoughts, noticing their impact on our health and our lives, we can exercise our power of choice. We can choose to let go of negative thinking, adopt new habits of positive thinking and adapt our patterns of belief to suit our true needs and desires. It takes patience and practice, but every one of us has the power to transform our mental patterns. We can all adopt new thoughts and beliefs that are magnetic to positive, healthy experiences.

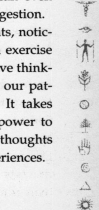

CHANGING OUR THOUGHTS

When we feel stuck, unhappy, depleted or distressed there is always something we can do to make a difference: we can change the thought. We can ask ourselves *'What is the belief that is contributing to this problem?'*, or *'How are my thoughts affecting my feelings, depleting my energy and inhibiting my ability to grow?'* We can learn to listen to our thoughts, notice the impact that they have on our lives and make the choice to change them.

When we are sick we can take positive action by subscribing to the appropriate medical or complementary treatments that are available to us, but this is not the only thing that we have it in our power to do. We can take the time to notice the thoughts and beliefs that could be contributing to our condition and change them to thoughts that will support our treatments and stimulate or, in some cases, accelerate the healing process.

When we are having problems in our relationships we can ask ourselves *'Have I learned to think, act or respond in ways that could be contributing to these problems?'* The way that we think about relationships in general, the beliefs that we hold about people of the opposite sex, people of the same sex, our sexuality, our bodies and our self-esteem all contribute to the kinds of relationship that we create. If we do not like what we are creating we may need to change the thought.

We can begin to notice our thoughts and beliefs by listening to the language that we use. What words do you use again and again when you are on the telephone, talking to your parents, talking to your children, talking to your partner, conversing with a colleague or making small talk with someone that you have just met? Do you complain about the state of the world? Do you criticize yourself or other people? Do you talk about the things that are limiting you or lacking in your life? Do you use 'struggle words' such as *hard*, *difficult* or *trying*? Do you use compulsive words such as *ought*, *must* and *should*?

The more that we listen to ourselves talking, the more we can begin to notice the negative or limiting conversations that we have during the course of the day and the easier it is to pinpoint some of our underlying negative or limiting beliefs.

Exercise: Mind your Language

Take a day to listen to the language that you use. Is the main content of your conversation negative or positive? Are you critical, blaming and quick to judge or are you generally accepting, supportive and compassionate when you talk about yourself and other people? Do you talk about life in a way that is fearful or that expects failure or do you use words that invite safety, positive opportunities and success? Is your language filled with struggle words? Do you talk about how hard your life is or do you talk about the ease and joy of life?

If it helps, carry a pen and notebook around with you so that you can record anything that you notice about your choice of words and ideas. Alternatively, leave a tape recorder switched on for periods of time so that you can forget it is there and allow yourself to talk as you normally would.

Perhaps you will discover that the things you say are constantly negative. Some people are amazed when they do this exercise because they generally believe themselves to be quite positive and have not previously noticed the mass of negative or limiting words, phrases and concepts that they utter. Even genuinely positive people may pinpoint negative patterns of thought that they are still carrying with them from their childhood or from some period of frustration or disappointment that they have had in their lives.

If you do not notice very much, do not worry, it takes practice to listen to ourselves. Pinpointing even just one thing can begin a powerful process of transformation. Here is a guide to some common words or phrases that may help you.

STRUGGLE WORDS

Our parents may have told us, either directly or indirectly, that life is hard. As children we copied the language that they and other key figures in our formative lives constantly used. If that language included words, phrases, sayings or concepts that expressed the difficulty of life, then it is highly likely that our language will also express our deeply held belief in difficulty and struggle.

Struggle words are burdening. They weigh us down mentally, emotionally and physically, leaving us feeling dispirited and making us magnetic to difficulty in all areas of our lives. Beliefs in struggle contribute to physical tension, in some cases making our bodies look and feel defeated or joyless. They can inhibit us from having our needs met and can frustrate our ability to create the health, prosperity or relationships that we truly desire.

Here are some examples of struggle words, concepts or phrases that many of us use:

- Hard

- Difficult

- Trying

- Struggle

- Hard work

- Crisis

- Disaster.

'It is difficult for me to learn new things.'

'I am in a difficult situation.'

'It will take hard work to achieve that.'

'I always work hard but it never seems to get me anywhere.'

'It is always such a struggle to make ends meet.'

'I am trying to change but it is a struggle.'

'I can't win.'

'It is hard for me to change.'

'This is such a crisis.'

'It is always such a disaster.'

If we are constantly telling ourselves how hard or difficult life is, how can we expect it to get any easier?

COMPULSIVE WORDS

As children, we also learn compulsive words from the people around us. Whenever we are told that we *must* do something, that we really *ought* to do it and that it is something that really *should* be done, we create compulsive beliefs – particularly when words like must, ought and should are repeated to us often. We copy compulsive beliefs from parent figures who constantly talk about what we, they or other people ought, must or should do.

Compulsive words create and reinforce compulsive beliefs that are often frustrating, draining and inhibiting. They act by motivating us to do things in a way that is pressured and joyless. The result is that we often push ourselves to the limit or more often give up in the attempt to reach some unhealthy measure of success or self-worth. Either way there is a feeling of failure and we come to feel bad about ourselves or to punish ourselves for our lack of success.

Compulsive words limit our choices. We use compulsive beliefs to drive ourselves too hard, push ourselves to do things that we do not want to do and in some cases force ourselves into situations that are unhealthy or damaging for us. They can contribute to desperation, workaholic tendencies, depression, laziness and fatigue.

Here are some examples of compulsive words, concepts or phrases that many of us use:

- Must/Must not

- Ought/Ought not

- Should/Should not

- Have to.

As in:

'I must try harder to succeed.'

'I must not stop until I have finished.'

'I have to do this before I can do the things that I want to do.'

'I should not cry in front of other people.'

'I should stick to my diet.'

'I ought to be feeling better by now.'

'If I can just do this then everything will be all right.'

Some of the things that we think or talk about compulsively may be healthy for us to do. Perhaps we would benefit from sticking to our diet, but it is the way that we are thinking about it that is unhealthy. Compulsive thinking can inhibit, frustrate or sabotage the success of good, healthy schemes by rendering them joyless and turning them into a chore or a punishment.

FEARFUL PHRASES

Most of us also develop a vocabulary of fearful phrases, some exactly the same as those that we learned in childhood, others that we have picked up, adapted and created for ourselves in adult life. Fearful phrases create and reinforce fearful beliefs. At their extreme we use them to paralyse ourselves and render us inactive and impotent. Fear is a natural feeling, but fearful phrases stir us up into a terrified state that is unnatural and unhealthy.

The stress and anxiety caused by fearful thinking can lower the immune system, disrupt our natural ability to protect ourselves psychologically or mentally, raise our blood-pressure and impede our ability to enjoy the pleasures of life. The energy of fearful beliefs can even make us magnetic to the outcomes that we most wish to avoid. What we resist persists!

Here are some examples of the fearful phrases that many of us use:

'You can't trust anyone these days.'

'I would be terrified of making a fool of myself.'

'We live in a dangerous world.'

'These are dangerous times.'

'It is not safe to walk the streets any more.'

'If the crooks don't get you the government will.'

'I'll dry up in the middle of my exam and forget everything that I've learned.'

'What if I make a mistake?'

'It is terrifying!'

'What a nightmare!'

Like any other negative patterns, our fearful words and thoughts are just bad habits, and bad habits can easily be changed. We just need to be willing to change them.

NEGATIVE AND LIMITING EXPECTATIONS

Fearful beliefs are just one form of negative or limiting expectations. Our language is full of phrases and statements that reveal underlying expectations of failure, disappointment, disaster and loss. When we expect the worst we become like a character in a story or a play who carries within him a negative self-fulfilling prophesy of how his life will develop. Our negative expectations are fatalistic. They paint us as victims of tragedy or mishap rather than as the masters of our own destiny with the power to take charge of our health and happiness.

Here are some examples of phrases that reveal our negative or limiting expectations:

'Why should I bother, it will never work.'

'I'll only be disappointed.'

'I'll make myself ill doing this.'

'They will be glad to see the back of me.'

'It will only get worse.'

'I'll never make any money.'

'Nothing good will ever come of it.'

'You can have too much of a good thing.'

'I take one step forward and two steps back.'

'I have got to make the best of a bad job.'

'It will end in tears.'

Just as we can create a negative self-fulfilling prophecy in our lives, we can create a positive one. Changing our language, changing our thoughts and transforming our underlying beliefs can powerfully change the reality of our health, well-being, emotional state, relationships, career, finances and spiritual evolution.

YOUR INNER VOICES

Listening to the words and phrases that you use when you talk is just one key to noticing your thoughts and beliefs. There are many times during the day when we are not in conversation with somebody else. These are moments when we can be most aware of our inner dialogue. Our minds are constantly thinking. We have thousands and thousands of thoughts every day of our lives; we need to begin to listen to our inner voices as they chatter away to us.

It can take practice to listen to our thoughts. Even when we are on our own we can create enough noise and activity around us to drown out our inner voices, and sometimes they are just so familiar to us that we do not hear them. Many of our thoughts may be positive, but just like the sentiments that we express aloud we may also have numerous words, phrases or

concepts going around and around in our minds that are negative, limiting, fearful, compulsive or filled with conflict and
struggle.

Exercise: Listening to your Inner Voices

Take ten minutes of silence to listen to your inner voices. Make
sure that you are on your own and minimize distractions by
unplugging the telephone, turning off radios and television
sets or anything else that may drown out your thoughts and
distract you from your task. It is often best to find a comfortable
spot where you can sit upright, your body open and relaxed
and your feet placed firmly on the floor in front of you.

For anyone who is unused to stillness and silence it may feel
uncomfortable to do this for the first time. For some of us, the
only time we stop rushing around is when we sleep, and it is
possible that you may feel drowsy and want to nod off. This is
why it is better to do this sitting upright. If you find yourself
getting sleepy or, alternatively, looking for distractions, just
bring your attention gently back to what you are doing and
continue to listen to your thoughts.

Notice any positive voices. Notice the negative ones. Is your
mind quite busy or is it still? Do you have fearful thoughts? Do
you think about all of the things that you *should* be doing? Are
your inner voices doubtful, happy, anxious, peaceful or confused? Are you full of negative or positive expectations?

When you complete your ten minutes' of stillness, return to
your normal tasks and activities of the day but see if you can
continue to notice your thoughts as you do so. Every so often,
pause during your activities and ask yourself *'What am I thinking now?'* Do your best to keep this going for as long as you can:
notice your thoughts as you work, eat, rest, bathe, shop, watch
television, travel, undress or settle down to sleep at night.
Notice your inner voices when you first wake up. Are they pos-

itive? Are they negative? Do they support you in health and happiness? Do you need to change them?

The more that you can practise listening to and noticing your thoughts, the easier it will be to heal your mind and change your life for the better.

SO HOW DO WE CHANGE OUR THOUGHTS?

When we bring our awareness to bear on some aspect of our lives or our behaviour we automatically begin a process of transformation. When we notice the things that we do or say that do not serve us we often start to change them as a matter of course. The same is true for our negative or limiting thoughts. Perhaps our willingness to listen to them is a symptom of some inner spark of healing that we carry within us, an aspect of ourselves that is always growing and changing regardless of our conscious choices.

Noticing begins a process of change that is similar to shining a torch ahead of us as we walk down a dark path. Because we can see where we are going and what we might be about to step in we automatically pick our route with greater care and accuracy. However, because we are receiving more information about our path forward we also have the raw material with which to make some conscious and radical changes of direction. If the path does not take us where we most want to go we can choose another one or carve out a completely new and untrodden route. Noticing our thoughts, there is much that we can do to stimulate or accelerate the process of change.

POSITIVE REFUSAL

We can simply refuse to think or say negative or limiting things. Whenever you catch yourself saying something that is critical or fearful you can gently stop yourself and refuse to continue. There are times when it will serve you better to remain silent than to engage in a conversation with another person that will trigger your negative patterns of thought.

You can gently stop your thoughts mid-flow, treating them like invitations that you are gracefully refusing to accept. In your mind, you could say to yourself: *'Thank you, I now choose to be positive.'*

If it helps, you can imagine that your negative thoughts have an 'off' button and you can simply picture yourself turning them off so that you can choose to do something more pleasurable. This can be like turning off an old record that no longer gives you pleasure and choosing to listen to something new instead.

RADIATING LOVE

The most effective way of transforming our negative thoughts is to treat them with love and compassion. If we hate them then we make ourselves available to thoughts of self-hatred and can create a pattern of inner conflict, combat and tension that both adds to our negative energy and keeps us attached to the very patterns that we are wishing to release.

I have heard people talk about 'fighting' their negativity or 'combating' their disease, and while this often reflects their courage and commitment it is based on beliefs that can reinforce negative patterns or contribute to disease. We need to think in terms of gentle refusal, release, change and transformation rather than of getting rid of our negativity, destroying our limiting beliefs or obliterating our illness. Our most powerful gift for healing negativity is our innate ability to love.

You could imagine your negative or limiting beliefs as scared or unhappy children who need a little extra love. Every time you hear yourself thinking or saying something negative, stop yourself and imagine that the thought and the underlying belief are being radiated with love which instantly transforms them into positivity, happiness and contentment. With love, a fearful thought can become one of positive anticipation.

On days when you find that you are being particularly negative about yourself or the people around you, it may be valuable to take a sideways step and give yourself some reassurance. Just as you might reassure and comfort a frightened or angry child, you can say to yourself: *'You are safe. I love you and will always take care of you.'*

FINDING REPLACEMENTS

The simple act of replacing a negative thought with a positive one is an essential part of any healing transformation. It makes sense that if we let go of negative beliefs that are not supporting us we are going to need to create a new vocabulary of positive thoughts and beliefs that do. If we choose to release the patterns that are contributing to our illness or disharmony then we also need to take on thoughts that help us to create health, well-being and success.

The additional gift of positive thinking is that it automatically displaces, dissolves and releases our deeply held negative patterns. When we repeat a positive thought over and over in our minds it does not allow space for the negative voices to take hold; it fills us with a positive energy that washes away the old negativity. The more we use a positive thought, the more it can release us from old, negative associations and the more the habit of negativity can be replaced with one of love, health and positive anticipation.

Whenever you notice yourself thinking a negative thought you can stop it before it takes hold and replace it with a thought that is joyful, life-affirming and healthy. Within the next chapter we will be learning how to choose and use the power of positive thought. Most people who are willing to heal their thinking are amazed at the impact that their new positive thoughts have on their lives and well-being. We just need to be willing to change our lives for the better.

For now, repeat the following positive statement to yourself and remember to use it whenever you notice yourself slipping into old, negative thought patterns:

- MY MIND IS FILLED WITH POSITIVE, HEALTHY THOUGHTS.

and take a few moments with me to wash away the impact of those negative and limiting thoughts...

Visualization: The Waterfall

Find somewhere quiet and comfortable to sit, unplug the telephone and make sure that you are not going to be disturbed. Sit with your back supported, your body open and relaxed with your arms and legs uncrossed. If you prefer you can lie down for this, but again make sure that you keep your body open rather than curled up.

As before, I am going to invite you to use some positive mental imagery. Some people have strong images when they do this, some do not. It is enough, however, to hold the idea or concept in your mind for this exercise to work for you.

To begin, breathe deeply and imagine that you are standing beside a beautiful waterfall on a hot summer's day. The air around you is clean and fresh and there is a slight heat haze. There is something else, too: This place has a special, magical quality; there is an atmosphere of healing that you can almost touch.

Below the waterfall is a pool where the water collects. It all looks so inviting that you discard your clothes and step in. See yourself wading through the coolness of the pool and approaching the heart of the waterfall. Imagine yourself stepping into it and showering in the softly cascading waters, your body tingling with refreshment and a feeling of aliveness.

Imagine the water cleansing and discharging any old, negative energy; all your old fears, pain, discomfort and stress dissolve away harmlessly. Imagine too that the water washes away any old, negative thoughts, releasing you from patterns of belief that do not support your health, well-being and joy. Imagine any areas of disease, disharmony and distress flowing away from you in the clear, magical waters.

When you feel complete, see yourself emerging from the waterfall and wading to the edge of the pool, feeling recharged and rejuvenated. Picture yourself stepping out of the water and drying off in the warm air. When you go to dress again, you discover that your clothes have been replaced by a beautiful new set that feel wonderful to wear.

Repeat this visualization regularly. If it helps, you could make a recording of your own voice to guide you through it or, alternatively, take turns with a friend to guide the visualization and be guided through it.

You could also imagine your old, negative thoughts washing harmlessly away whenever you physically bathe or shower. Every time you gently cleanse your body there is an opportunity for you to let go of the past and think of yourself as clean, fresh and positive in each new moment.

YOUR POSITIVE POTENTIAL

HEALTHY THOUGHTS

ealthy thoughts are permissive thoughts. They permit us to be who we truly are. When we believe positive, healthy things about ourselves and about life we allow ourselves the freedom, joy, pleasure and peace of mind that we truly deserve. Healthy thinking brings with it self-acceptance, self-approval and self-love.

Have you ever looked at someone and seen the wonderful, healthy, special person shining out from within while also seeing the confusion, negativity, disease, disharmony or conflict that is around him or her? We are all like this to some extent, beautiful, healthy beings within that have become partially obscured by some of the negative baggage of our lives: the illnesses, the problems, the hurtful experiences and, chiefly, the negative or limiting beliefs.

Healthy, positive thinking allows our inner spark of light and vitality to become more visible and more active so that it is the true healthy nature of our being, and not the negative baggage, that is directing the course of our lives. Imagine a brilliant golden sunshine that is partially obscured by a blanket of smog. The sunlight will always be there regardless of the smog, but its full

impact can only be felt when the smog has been cleared away. Positive thinking clears away the smog of negativity so that our full, creative brilliance can be visible and active.

RETRAINING THE MIND

Just as we learned to think in certain ways when we were children, we can learn to think in new ways now. Have you noticed how small children love to copy things? Most of the childhood training that we received worked by repetition. Phrases, statements, reactions and patterns of behaviour were repeated to us and around us until we started to copy them and repeat them internally. We allowed them to imprint on our minds as thoughts and then as basic beliefs. As we developed, we continued to repeat these beliefs to ourselves, adding more layers of thought and belief to them as we absorbed more information from the world around us.

One of the reasons that we are sometimes oblivious to our patterns of negative belief is that we learned to identify with them very powerfully from an early age. It is understandable, therefore, that they feel natural to us. They have coloured our view of the world for most of our lives and they strongly influence our interpretation of each new experience. Even the most absurd beliefs can seem true for us because they have been attached to us for so long.

The good news is that it does not matter how much we have learned to identify with a negative or limiting belief, by retraining our minds we can replace that belief with one that is much healthier. We can learn to identify with ideas that reflect our new, positive view of ourselves. We can dissolve the negative influences from the past and make ourselves available to new, positive experiences. The key is very simple: positive repetition.

If you are a person who uses a lot of struggle words and you are constantly telling yourself how hard or how difficult everything is, then finding the appropriate positive thoughts, words, phrases or statements to repeat instead will dissolve these negative patterns. Instead of saying, *'It is difficult for me to manage'* whenever a task is proving stressful or challenging, you can acknowledge the challenge, look for new solutions and repeat to yourself, *'It is easy for me to manage.'*

This new statement of ease allows for solutions that you may have been blocking with your negative thoughts. It sends out a magnetic energy that makes you more available to the right kind of help, new insights, new methods or alternative ways of achieving the same goal. It is our thoughts that make us available for either difficulty or ease, crisis or opportunity, struggle or grace; the repetition of positive, easy thoughts powerfully shifts our availability.

Isobel came to me complaining about problems in her marriage. She and her husband had been married for ten years, and during that time she had felt increasingly unsupported and unloved by him although she knew that he was committed to their relationship. She had a part-time job, looked after their children when they were not at school and was responsible for most of the household management. Her husband had a full-time job, was supportive in providing for his family financially but would never make a decision about anything other than work and would often be absent when there were things to be done around the home and she needed his help.

Isobel had frequent backaches and headaches, which would increase in frequency whenever she had to make important decisions or when the pressure of her workload built up. She constantly told me how hard her life was, saying *'It is so difficult to get everything done'* and *'It is so hard to get my husband to do anything at home.'* Most frequently she would say, *'I struggle to do it on my own'* or *'I struggle to make the right decision.'* I asked her whether she talked to her husband about their situation and her feelings. Her reply was, *'It is difficult for me to talk about things, I am not very good at it.'*

I suggested to Isobel that she was co-creating the situation with her husband and that if she wanted to heal the relationship it would benefit her to think about it in a different way and to open some new areas of communication between them. I also suggested that she and her husband might benefit from relationship counselling if he were willing to attend counselling sessions with her. To begin with, I gave her a collection of positive thoughts to use so that she could retrain herself to be available for solutions. These included:

- **IT IS EASY FOR ME TO COMMUNICATE.**

- **IT IS EASY FOR ME TO ASK FOR HELP.**

- **I AM ALWAYS SUPPORTED IN MAKING DECISIONS.**

- IT IS EASY FOR ME TO HAVE MY NEEDS MET.

- LIFE SUPPORTS ME FULLY.

- MY LIFE IS SIMPLE AND EASY.

Isobel decided that she would start with changing her thoughts and then progress to talking with her husband about her feelings and frustrations. We planned to spend our next meeting as a rehearsal period for her to practise methods of opening up a dialogue with her husband; I was to help her role-play new ways of asking for her needs to be met that were not cluttered up with blame and recrimination. Events did not turn out exactly as we had planned.

Within three days of using her new, positive thoughts, Isobel found herself on her own with her husband for a couple of hours while their children were playing next door. She felt an overwhelming urge to start talking to him about how she felt, but before she could utter a word he said, *'Are you all right? You seem really distant these days.'* Isobel immediately burst into tears and they started to talk in a way that they had never done before. They were still talking two hours later when their children returned.

Isobel's husband did not immediately understand everything that she said to him, but he was concerned about her and realized that his lack of support was contributing to her distress. He recognized that there was more that he could do to support her and that he had not been taking an equal share of their practical responsibilities and decisions. However, he also told her that one reason he had backed off was that she constantly criticized the things that he had done in the past and she had frequently undermined him when he had made decisions. What is more, he often left her to get on with things because she made even the simplest of tasks seem such hard work.

Isobel continued to use her positive thoughts and she and her husband made a commitment to do more things together and to keep talking. Although her husband was initially resistant, they even started to go for relationship counselling and their lives steadily improved. Isobel's headaches and backaches got better and she began to enjoy the ease and fun of life. It is true that she still had a busy life, but she was now able to let her hair down a bit and realize that she did not have to turn everything into hard work.

CHOOSING YOUR POSITIVE THOUGHTS

The choice of which positive thoughts to use will depend upon your changing needs, desires and aspirations. If you are dealing with a physical condition then you are going to need positive thoughts that can support you in healing or managing your symptoms and addressing the underlying cause of your illness. If you are wishing to prevent illness then you need positive thoughts that reinforce your natural, healthy state and create expectations of future health and well-being.

Positive thoughts are at their most transformational when they are specifically tailored to counter, displace and dissolve the negative or limiting thought patterns that we currently have. Our negative thoughts contain the raw material for our new, positive ones. They provide us with many clues to our illnesses or problems, and therefore to our solutions. Some of the most effective, positive thoughts are those that are directly opposite to the thoughts and beliefs that we have carried around with us for most of our lives.

TRANSFORMING STRUGGLE THOUGHTS

With Isobel's story we saw how she began to turn around some of her basic beliefs in struggle and hard work using positive thoughts that ran counter to her old, negative patterns. Here are some more examples of how to transform struggle words, concepts or phrases:

The words *hard* and *difficult* can become *easy*, as in:

'It is easy for me to learn new things.'

'My life constantly becomes easier.'

The words *crisis* and *disaster* can become *opportunity* or *challenge*:

'This is such an opportunity.'

'It is a challenge for me but it continues to get easier.'

The phrase *'I can't'* can become *'I can'*:

'I can win!'

The word *trying* can become *doing my best*:

'I am doing my best to change.'

'Trying' is a word that adds tension and confusion to anything that we are choosing to do. It creates an energy of frustration, impotence and disempowerment. We either choose to do something or we choose not to; if we have yet to succeed at least we can acknowledge ourselves for doing our best.

TRANSFORMING COMPULSIVE THOUGHTS

Transforming compulsive thoughts comes with adopting the language of choice. We need to think about our actions and responses as choices that we are making and that we can change if they no longer suit us or if they do not support our health and well-being.

Here are some examples of how to transform compulsive words, concepts or phrases:

Must and *must not* can become *may* and *may not*:
'*I may choose to do more.*'
'*I may not choose to stop.*'

Ought and *should* can become *choose* and *could*:
'*I could choose to stick to my diet.*'
'*I could be feeling better by now.*'

Ought not and *should not* can become *choose not*:
'*I choose not to cry in front of other people.*'

With this example, the language of choice allows us to be open to releasing our negative or limiting beliefs about crying in front of other people. We can learn that it is safe to express our feelings and be seen to be emotional in front of others if we choose to rather than be stuck with the emotional straitjacket of a thought like, '*I should not cry in front of other people.*'

Have to can become *choose to*:
'*I choose to do this job before I do the other things that I want to do.*'

'*I choose to find another solution.*'

TRANSFORMING FEARFUL THOUGHTS

The most powerful word for transforming fearful thoughts is the word *safe*. When we acknowledge our fears, reassure ourselves that we are safe and release our fearful thoughts, we make ourselves available for new, safer experiences. A belief in safety can help to make us magnetic to the outcomes that we most desire, it can fill and surround us with a calming, healthy and protective energy that makes it easier for us to be ourselves.

Here are some examples of how to transform the fearful thoughts and concepts that many of us have:

'You can't trust anyone these days' can become,
'It is safe and easy for me to trust other people.'

'I would be terrified of making a fool of myself' can become,
'It is safe for me to be myself.'

'We live in a dangerous world' or 'These are dangerous times'
can become,
'I am safe in the world.'

'It is not safe to walk the streets any more' can become,
'I am always safe, wherever I walk.'

'I'll dry up in the middle of my exam and forget everything that
I've learned' can become,
'I trust myself to do my best.'

'What if I make a mistake?' can become,
'It is OK to make mistakes.'

'It is terrifying!' and 'What a nightmare!' can become,
'It is challenging but I know that I am safe' and
'What an opportunity!'

Of course, when we recognize that we are in a situation where we are not physically safe, we need to take the responsible action of getting ourselves away from there as quickly as possible. Beliefs in safety work on at least two levels: as well as making us magnetic to safer experiences they can help us to think more clearly about what is safe and what is not, and activate our ability to deal with potentially threatening situations.

There is a huge difference between going for a job interview and being with a violent or abusive person, but to listen to our thoughts and beliefs sometimes you would not think so. Our fearful thoughts can make even the smallest things feel life-threatening and our bodies often respond with depleted immunity and ill health. Choosing positive, healthy beliefs can release us from negative, fearful energy and make us as safe as possible in all situations.

TRANSFORMING NEGATIVE AND LIMITING EXPECTATIONS

Instead of having a negative self-fulfilling prophecy, we need to create a positive one where we reinforce an expectation that our lives will be filled with positive, healthy, loving experiences. We need to paint ourselves as the masters of our own destiny, not necessarily able or needing to control every aspect of our lives but positively directing ourselves to people, situations and outcomes that are healthy and happy for us.

Here are some examples of how to transform our negative or limiting expectations into positive ones:

> *'Why should I bother, it will never work'* can become,
> *'I am always magnetic to success.'*
>
> *'I'll only be disappointed'* can become,
> *'Life continues to delight and satisfy me.'*
>
> *'I'll make myself ill doing this'* can become,
> *'I am always in perfect health.'*
>
> *'They will be glad to see the back of me'* can become,
> *'I am loved and appreciated wherever I go.'*
>
> *'It will only get worse'* can become,
> *'My life gets better all the time.'*
>
> *'I will never make any money'* can become,
> *'It is easy for me to make money.'*

'Nothing good will ever come of it' can become,
'Only good will come of this.'

'You can have too much of a good thing' can become,
'It is safe and easy for me to receive an abundance of good things.'

'I take one step forward and two steps back' can become,
'I always step forward into better and better experiences.'

'I have got to make the best of a bad job' can become,
'My creativity always brings me the best things in life.'

'It will end in tears' can become,
'I trust my life to be joyful and fulfilling.'

AFFIRMING OUR POSITIVE POTENTIAL

Phrases or statements that are used to retrain our minds to think positively are called positive affirmations. Many of the examples listed above would work fine as affirmations. They do not always have to be specifically related to an area of negative thought that we have noticed in ourselves for us to use them to great effect, they just need to be appropriate to our needs and desires.

We can use affirmations to help us to heal and to help us to stay healthy. Some examples of health affirmations that we would all benefit from using are:

- I AM ALWAYS HEALTHY AND BALANCED.

- MY LIFE IS FILLED WITH HEALTHY, LOVING EXPERIENCES.

- MY BODY GETS HEALTHIER EVERY DAY.

The key to using affirmations is to focus on our positive potential, be aware of our needs and desires and choose positive statements that help us to manifest that potential. If we are sick and we want to be well, we affirm for health; if we wish for emotional well-being, financial success, healthy relationships or spiritual growth, we need to choose the appropriate affirmations to help us.

Exercise: Creating a Vision of Health

Take some time to think about your own personal vision of health. What is your current state of physical, mental and emotional well-being? How would you like that to change and improve? If you are healthy you may need to develop a vision of staying healthy. If you are sick you may need to develop a vision of recuperation and a return to full health.

If you are dealing with an ongoing condition that brings you discomfort, pain, restriction and distress you may need a vision of managing your symptoms successfully, reducing pain and creating a better quality of life. Even if you are dealing with a potentially life-threatening illness it would benefit you to develop a healing vision and affirm for health, grace and peace of mind. Take a pen and paper and respond to these questions as thoroughly and definitively as you can:

- What is your current state of physical health?
  Include all of your symptoms and everything you know about your condition.

- How would you like your physical health to improve?
  Be specific – If you want to be released from pain, write it down; if you are quite healthy and want to stay that way, write it down.

- What is your current state of emotional health?

How do you currently feel inside?
Are you comfortable with your feelings?
Are you able to express your emotions safely and effectively?

- How would you like your emotional health to improve?
Would you like to feel differently?
Would you like to be happier?
Do you need to feel, express or balance your emotions?

- What is your current state of mental health?
Does your mind feel balanced and clear?
Could you be more positive?
Do you get confused?
Do you need to learn to switch your mind off at times so that you can relax?
Are you full of fears and self-doubts?

- How would you like your mental health to improve?
Would you like to think with greater clarity?
Would you like to create peace of mind?

Leave space to add any more ideas or thoughts that you may have later. When you are setting out on a path of self-healing it helps to be clear about where it is you want to go even if you do not yet know how to get there. With these ideas you can tailor-make some powerful positive affirmations to help you.

HOW TO CREATE AFFIRMATIONS

To create successful affirmations it helps to follow some basic guidelines.

- Affirmations need to be phrased in the present tense. For example, 'I NOW CREATE ...' (present simple tense) or 'I

AM ALWAYS ...' (Present continuous tense). If you affirm for something as if it is already true for you, then your mind can more readily make the changes that will alter your experience of life. However, if you affirm that something is *going* to happen or that it *will* happen, then you are creating it in the future and that is where it will stay, constantly out of reach. *'In three weeks I will be...'* will always stay three weeks away.

• Affirmations often work best when they are relatively short and easy to remember, so that you will be able to repeat them frequently. As I have mentioned before, repetition is the key to retraining the mind!

• In most cases affirmations need to be positively focused on your desired outcome rather than focused on the situations or conditions that you want to release. For example *'I am healthy and relaxed'* is a much more effective affirmation than *'I am never sick or tense.'* The latter will keep your attention unduly focused on the negative outcome, continuing to make it a reality in your life.

• Your negative or limiting thoughts are the raw material for creating positive affirmations. Each negative thought contains the foundation for positive change and growth. *'I will never be free of back pain'* can become *'My back is free, healthy and comfortable.'*

Exercise: Creating your own Affirmations
With the help of your list of current health needs and vision of future improvement, create some positive thoughts to support you. Here are some examples to help:

Problems	*Vision*
Backaches, bad posture, tension in the lower back and in the shoulders.	To be pain free and physically comfortable with good posture and no tension in the back.

Affirmations:

- MY BACK IS ALWAYS HEALTHY.

- MY POSTURE CONSTANTLY IMPROVES.

- MY BACK IS ALWAYS FLEXIBLE AND STRONG.

- I AM ALWAYS RELAXED AND COMFORTABLE.

- MY BACK MOVES WITH EASE AND COMFORT.

- MY SHOULDERS ARE ALWAYS RELAXED.

- MY LOWER BACK IS HEALTHY AND FREE.

- I FILL MY BACK WITH LOVE AND HEALING.

You will notice that these affirmations fit the guidelines. They are short, written in the present or present continuous tense and focus upon the desired outcome rather than on the problem that is to be released. Rather than affirming for no more back pain we are affirming for comfort, relaxation, flexibility and ease.

Problems	*Vision*
Breast cancer, tiredness, distress, fear of undergoing treatment for breast cancer.	Complete physical and emotional health, complete remission from cancer, peace of mind, renewed energy, a feeling of aliveness, a comfortable, safe and peaceful process of treatment.

- THE CELLS OF MY BODY ARE ALWAYS HEALTHY.

- MY BREASTS ARE HEALTHY AND WHOLE.

- I FILL MY BREASTS WITH HEALING ENERGY.

- MY BODY RE-CREATES ITSELF IN HEALTH AND VITALITY.

- MY ENERGY IS REGENERATED AND RENEWED.

- I AM PHYSICALLY AND EMOTIONALLY HEALTHY.

- IT IS SAFE FOR ME TO BE ALIVE.

- I AM ALWAYS TREATED WITH THE UTMOST CARE AND LOVE.

- I AM MAGNETIC TO THE BEST TREATMENTS.

- MY PROCESS OF HEALING IS COMFORTABLE AND SAFE.

- MY MIND IS PEACEFUL.

There are many more affirmations that could be created to help with these needs and this healing vision. Perhaps you can think of some. As well as fitting the guidelines it is important that they address your individual needs.

Problems	*Vision*
Depression, lethargy, lack of motivation, lack of direction, fear of making decisions.	Joy, motivation and aliveness. A clear sense of direction and an ability to make the right decisions.

Affirmations:

- I AM SAFE WITH ALL OF MY FEELINGS.

- I FOLLOW MY HEART'S DESIRE.

- IT IS SAFE AND EASY FOR ME TO MAKE DECISIONS.

- I EASILY FIND MY CHOSEN PATH.

- MY DIRECTION IS ALWAYS CLEAR.

- I TRUST MYSELF TO MAKE THE RIGHT DECISIONS.

- I AM ALWAYS MOTIVATED AND INSPIRED.

- MY LIFE IS FILLED WITH JOY.

- MY FEELINGS ARE ALIVE AND JOYFUL.

Depression is often described as a flatness or an absence of feeling. Feelings are held in, denied, stuck or pushed down because we do not think that we have permission to have them or express them. It is not surprising that we may lose our motivation if we have feelings of anger, joy or sadness that we are not expressing or that we do not know how to express safely. When depressed, it may also help to affirm:

- I AM SAFE WITH MY ANGER.

- I AM SAFE WITH MY SADNESS.

- I AM SAFE WITH MY JOY.

- I EXPRESS ALL OF MY FEELINGS SAFELY AND EFFECTIVELY.

| Stomach cramps, indigestion, mental confusion during times of stress. | A healthy, comfortable stomach, ease of digestion and clear thinking. |

Affirmations:

- MY STOMACH IS HEALTHY AND COMFORTABLE.

- I DIGEST WITH EASE AND EFFICIENCY.

- I EASILY FIND THE CORRECT DIET FOR MY NEEDS.

- I AM MAGNETIC TO APPROPRIATE TREATMENTS AND THERAPIES.

- I AM ALWAYS RELAXED.

- I THINK CLEARLY.

- MY MIND IS ALWAYS POSITIVE AND CLEAR.

- I FILL MY STOMACH WITH HEALING LIGHT.

When you have completed creating your own list of affirmations, check once again that they address your needs and vision and that they fit the guidelines. Choose three or four of the most pertinent affirmations to begin with and read them through a few times to become familiar with them. Of course, you can use and benefit from all of the positive thoughts that you have created, but it helps to choose just a few that you will be able to remember wherever you are. Let us now look at the ways that we can use affirmations to transform our thoughts and experiences.

THE USE OF AFFIRMATIONS

- Affirmations can be written, typed, spoken aloud, sung, chanted and said to yourself in the mirror as well as being repeated over and over in your mind. Many people find that they benefit from filling their homes with affirmational thoughts, perhaps writing or painting them in bright colours and pasting them on the bathroom mirror, the fridge, on the doors or anywhere else where they will be constantly visible. Be creative and choose ways to use them that work best for you.

- Affirmations are wonderful when they are used in conjunction with meditation or physical exercise. Choosing one or two affirmations and repeating them silently to yourself in your mind, with the rhythm of your breath or in time to the repetition of a familiar exercise, can help them to become second nature. You may even repeat affirmations in your mind as you walk, pacing them out with every step that you take.

- Affirmations can easily be recorded for you to listen to while you are meditating, relaxing, having a bath, pottering around your home, travelling to work or at any other time. You could make a tape by getting a trusted friend or family member to speak your chosen series of positive thoughts into a tape recorder. Ask them to include your name from time to time so that it is as personally tailored to you as possible. Even more powerful would be a recording of your own voice speaking the affirmations; again put your own name into some of the positive statements. For example, *'I, David, am always healthy and happy'* or *'Janine, you are always safe and protected.'* You may choose to build up a collection of tapes to use over and over again.

- Although it is wonderful to set aside some special time every day or every couple of days to focus on your affirmations, you do not have to view them as yet another task to fit into your busy schedule. Perhaps the best way to use them is to make them an integral part of your life. You could affirm on your way to and from work, while you are cooking the dinner, while you are doing the housework or going through your morning routine. Perhaps the best times to do affirmations include those last few minutes at night just before you go to sleep and those first few minutes in the morning when you are still waking up. These are times when your mind is receptive and when you can influence your night's rest or the mood of your day ahead. After a time you may wake up with the positive thoughts already there in your mind, repeating themselves with brightness and clarity to welcome you to the day.

- Some of the best affirmations to use are those that run contrary to your current beliefs or differ greatly from what is presently real and true for you. For example, if you are sick then it may seem strange to affirm 'I am always in perfect health.' However, it will probably be one of the most appropriate positive statements to practise. Of course you do need to recognize what is happening to your body and to make appropriate choices about treatments; but while you are doing this the exercise of affirming for health will support your healing process and help the treatments you have chosen to work.

- Be patient with yourself. Your new positive thoughts may seem strange at first and could even feel false or phony because they are creating a new pattern of belief that is so totally at odds with the negative or limiting patterns that are familiar to you. Stepping out into new, positive territory can feel unreal or even scary.

- Remember, the biggest key to retraining your mind is repetition. The more you use affirmations, the more they can work for you. It is good to have a few favourite affirmations that you will always remember wherever you are, while at the same time frequently introducing your mind to new ones that address a particular need. You can never have too many positive thoughts, but when you are first introducing your mind to them it is perhaps better to have a few that you will be able to memorize and use than an endless list that can be easily forgotten.

- Affirmations are meant to be fun. Play with them, experiment with them and find ways to use them that are entertaining for you.

Continue to review your needs, enlarge upon your healing vision and use appropriate affirmations. The process of retraining the mind is ongoing and expansive. There is always value in affirming for the things that you desire.

THE INTELLIGENCE OF YOUR BODY

THE POWER OF YOUR BODY

Our bodies have an extraordinary capacity for self-healing. Whether we are sleeping or awake and preoccupied with the details of our day, our bodies are taking care of the digestion and assimilation of food, the elimination of waste matter, the assimilation of oxygen from the air and the continual regeneration of cells. There are many things that our bodies have to deal with, from infections to sprains and from cuts to bruises which in numerous cases will get better regardless of the treatments that we use. Our bodies know how to heal and regenerate themselves, they have their own intelligence.

Even in cases of disability or some long-term conditions that disrupt certain functions, the intelligence of the body is still able to take care of an incredible number of sophisticated tasks. Whatever our state of health, listening to and working with the intelligence of our bodies can make a significant difference to the speed of our recuperation and our ability to stay as healthy and as comfortable as possible.

GETTING IN THE WAY

Perhaps the main challenge that the body is likely to face as it goes about the business of regenerating itself comes from within. We have learned to get in the way of the body's natural ability to heal, obstructing many of its normal functions and inhibiting its natural rhythms and timing. How you think about your body and how you treat it often disrupts its ability to function as efficiently as it can.

In many cases we have become quite separated from our bodies. So much emphasis is placed upon our ability to think in logical, reasonable ways, to the exclusion of our intuition and gut awareness, that we cut off from much of the physical information that we receive. Intelligence has become chiefly associated with intellect; we have forgotten that our bodies also have intelligence. Harnessing that intelligence, listening to it, acknowledging it and responding to it are essential to self-healing.

Many of us have learned to hate our bodies. We send our bodies messages of self-loathing, abuse and mistrust. We have learned to fear our sexuality, despise the way that we look and criticize our bodies for their failings rather than acknowledge their strengths. We say things like, 'I hate my thighs,' 'My body is always letting me down' and 'I hate the way that I look.' Apart from the negative energy of all those negative thoughts, we give our bodies specific messages that they respond to. Is it any wonder that they sometimes respond with weakness, disharmony or disease?

We abuse our bodies with alcohol, nicotine and other recreational drugs and expect them to bounce back as if nothing had happened. The remarkable thing is that they often do bounce back, making an incredible effort to adjust to the effects of these poisonous substances and eliminate them from our systems.

However, the more that we abuse them in this way, the less that they will be able to bounce back until various functions become severely impaired or pack up completely. The good news is that as soon as we stop or significantly reduce our use of recreational drugs our bodies begin to clean and regenerate themselves.

We abuse our bodies with food. We eat too much or too little. We eat at odd or irregular times of the day. We eat too much junk food, too much processed food or too many food items that our bodies are intolerant to or allergic to. I do not believe that there is one ideal diet for us all. We are unique and our bodies have their own needs and rhythms. What is an excellent diet for one person may be quite wrong for another. What is more, our bodies may have different needs at different times during our lives; we would benefit from listening to these changing needs, noticing the impact that food has upon us, choosing to eat the foods that our bodies want and adapting our habits and lifestyle accordingly.

As a general rule, we are more likely to stay healthy when we have regular meal-times, eat wholefoods rather than junk, eat fresh foods rather than processed, tinned or frozen ones, eat lots of fresh vegetables and fruit, eat a balance of raw and cooked foods and avoid eating lots of cheese, red meat and processed sugar. Even the way that we think about what we eat can make a difference. If we think about our food positively before we put it in our mouths, our bodies can respond to it in a healthier way. However, even these general guidelines are not right for everyone; we each need to experiment for ourselves.

We do not exercise our bodies enough or we exercise them in the wrong way, pushing them to the limit with exercise routines that are unnatural. It is just as unhealthy to have a static lifestyle as it is to 'go for the burn'. It often works best to have a mixture of different kinds of exercise, some gentle, some more vigorous, some more contemplative, some more upbeat and fun. Walking is excellent; oriental systems such as yoga or tai chi are second to none when properly taught; swimming improves stamina and lung capacity; aerobic dance classes and weight-training sessions are also fine when properly supervised and when not taken to extremes. As with diet, we need to experiment and find out what suits our bodies.

While I am a great believer in subscribing to both medical and complementary forms of health care and using whatever treatments are appropriate to our needs, I have also observed that many of us have a tendency to look for a quick fix rather than give our bodies what they really want. So often we take a pill to keep going when our bodies are crying out for rest and relaxation, or we take medication to fix our symptoms rather than deal with the underlying cause of our illness.

Some of the medication that we use can actually inhibit our immune system from effectively dealing with the imbalance or infection itself. Some medications come with so-called 'side-effects' that give our bodies something else to contend with in addition to our illness. I am not saying that medication is not worth while in its place – indeed medical science has developed cures that would have seemed miraculous even 50 years ago – but we do need to use medicines with awareness and not bombard our bodies with antibiotics for every little thing.

How often do you moan about your body, despise it or neglect it? How often do you look for an instant fix when your body is craving sustained attention in order to heal? Just as we get in the way of the body's natural ability to heal itself, we can step out of the way and take a nurturing, supportive role that allows the body's intelligence to be at its most effective. Feeling guilty about the abusive things that we have done to our bodies is not going to help. We need to feel good about ourselves regardless of what we may have done in the past, and begin to make some new positive choices about how we treat our bodies now.

LEARNING TO LOVE YOUR BODY

The best way to change our habits is to start by learning to think about our bodies in a different way. Bodies that are thought about and talked about with love are much more likely to respond with health and balance. Instead of going on about being too fat, being too thin, hating your thighs, hating your height or moaning about the proportions of your body, you can redirect that negative energy into positive energy that can help you to stay healthy. Rather than spend time talking or thinking about the ways in which your body fails you, you can place your attention on the many successes of your body and give energy to the things that it does well.

What we place our attention upon grows. If we constantly think about our bodies as unreliable, ugly, hateful and inadequate then we significantly contribute to patterns of disharmony and deterioration. If, on the other hand, we acknowledge the changes that we would like to make in our physical state while loving and accepting our bodies as they are now, praising them for the many ways in which they function well and doing our best to take care of them, we will significantly contribute to new patterns of health, well-being and beauty.

I do not believe that we are all meant to be a certain size, shape or weight with the same physical abilities and strengths. Our bodies are meant to be different, we are all unique – but we all have one thing in common: when we learn to love and take care of our bodies we can increase their ability to function well. Some of us are meant to be fatter than others, some of us are born with disabilities that are not going to go away, but the way that we think about them and act towards them can be transformational. We can support our bodies in finding their ideal, healthy weight, increasing their range of mobility, staying comfortable and pain-free and giving us a great deal of pleasure.

CHRISTINE'S STORY

Christine was a woman who participated in a couple of my self-healing and personal development courses. She was quite beautiful, with long, shining hair, a clear, open face and a radiant smile. Although she was about four stone above the average weight for her height, she moved beautifully and did not indicate that she was unduly uncomfortable with her body.

During the courses, I and my co-leader Justin Carson placed a strong emphasis on learning to love ourselves, encouraging our participants to use affirmations, visualizations and practical techniques to strengthen the most important relationship that each of us has, the loving relationship that we create with ourselves. Christine responded well to these ideas.

Christine was a self-contained person who had a quiet presence that other people liked and responded to. In the way that many of us think about ourselves, I would guess that she did not realize how beautiful and lovable she was, but she was willing to learn to think about herself in more loving ways. During her time with us she became more radiant as she soaked in the positive messages that she was giving herself.

I did not see Christine for over two years after she finished our courses. Then one day she rang me up, out of the blue, to book a one-to-one healing and counselling session. She said that she had made many wonderful changes in her life and now she wanted to come back for a 'top up' to help her to decide on her next steps forward. When she arrived on my doorstep for her appointment I was amazed. She was still the beautiful person that we had known previously, but now she was even more radiant and she had lost nearly four stone in weight.

During her session, Christine told me what had happened. She had made no special effort to diet or undergo treatment for weight reduction. Instead, she had continued to affirm her love for herself and for her body and gently built up her self-confidence. The more that she loved and accepted herself as she was, the happier she became and the excess weight gradually dissolved. She found that her eating habits had improved but without her consciously denying or depriving herself of anything that she wanted. There were just some foods that she did not want to eat as much of as before and it was easier for her to listen to her body's needs than it used to be. Being loved and accepted by her, Christine's body had found its own balance.

Being overweight is not necessarily about over-eating. Many fat people that I know and love eat a great deal less than people half their size. There are many reasons for carrying excess weight, including the metabolic rate that we have inherited from our parents, the beliefs that we learn and the experiences that we have during childhood. The weight of negative thoughts, unexpressed emotions, hidden fears and suppressed passions can all contribute to excess weight. Some of us are also naturally healthier carrying a little more weight than we would be if we were an average size. For Christine, when she developed a relationship of love and peace with her body it was able to find its own natural level.

HOW TO LOVE YOUR BODY

Changing the way that we think about our bodies works in exactly the same way as changing any other set of negative or limiting thoughts. We need to listen to ourselves, notice the negative patterns and choose to replace them with positive ones that support us. Changing our negative thoughts about our physical appearance or capabilities will help us to adapt

our behaviour so that we treat our bodies with the love and care that they deserve. Here are some guidelines to help:

- Refuse to compare your body to others. We are often taught to be quite critical of our appearance by comparing ourselves to other people. We learn to look at somebody else and either feel superior or inadequate depending upon how we rate our appearance or our capabilities against theirs. If we are looking for it, there is always someone who is going to appear more beautiful, more handsome, fatter, thinner, stronger, more agile or more able than us; the ultimate pay-off is that we get to feel bad about ourselves and hate our bodies.

Your body is unique. If you refuse to enter into judgements and comparisons you will allow yourself to enjoy the beauty and brilliance of your body, encouraging it to grow in health, strength and capability.

- Look at your body in a full-length mirror and notice your thoughts and reactions. This is most effective when you are naked. Does your mind immediately become critical? Do you look for distractions and tear yourself away from your image as soon as you can? Does it upset, distress or disappoint you when you look at any area of your body, such as your thighs, your arms, your wrinkles, your spots or your damaged leg?

Practise looking at yourself with as much love as you can. Talk to your body using words of love and respect. Even if it seems a strange or even silly thing to do at first, you will benefit from looking at your reflection and saying to yourself:

- I LOVE MY BODY.

- I LOVE MY CHEST/ARMS/THIGHS/SKIN, etc.

- I ASK MY BODY TO STAY HEALTHY.

- I THANK MY BODY FOR STAYING HEALTHY.

- Learn to touch yourself with tenderness and love. Do not hit yourself, even in jest, as you could be reinforcing abusive patterns of thought and behaviour from your past. Touch yourself and regard yourself as you would if you were the most precious jewel in the universe. The truth is that you are!

- Learn to think positively about your sexuality. Most of us have picked up some negative baggage about sex and sexuality during our lives. Perhaps we have learned to fear our bodies and the sexual feelings that we have. Perhaps we picked up our parents' discomfort in talking about sex, or we may feel guilty for enjoying the pleasure of our bodies. Some of the following affirmations will directly help your ability to enjoy and appreciate your sexuality.

Affirmations for Loving your Body

- I FILL AND SURROUND MY BODY WITH LOVE.

- I BATHE MY BODY WITH LOVE AND ACCEPTANCE.

- I TRUST MY BODY.

- I LISTEN TO MY BODY WITH LOVE AND COMPASSION.

- I ALLOW MY BODY TO GUIDE ME TOWARDS PERFECT HEALTH.

- I ENJOY THE PLEASURES OF MY BODY.

- MY BODY EASILY ASSUMES ITS NATURAL, HEALTHY STATE.

- MY BODY IS ALWAYS THE PERFECT SHAPE AND SIZE FOR MY HEALTH AND HAPPINESS.

- I ACCEPT MY BODY AND TRUST IT TO HEAL ITSELF.

- I AM SAFE WITH MY SEXUALITY.

- I ENJOY THE SENSUALITY OF MY BODY.

TEN WAYS TO LOVE YOUR BODY

Here are just a few, simple ways that you can give love and care to your body on a regular basis. Not all of them will cost you money but they will all help to relieve stress, clear negative energy and help you to stay healthy.

1) Massage your own feet and hands. With a little cream, lotion or oil you can gently massage your feet and hands. It is extraordinary how much tension we hold in these areas. By stroking the skin, making circular movements with the tips of your fingers or thumbs and gently flexing the fingers and toes you can release tension from throughout your body and instil a feeling of well-being and peace. A book or a course that teaches you more about massage may help. There are many available.

2) Take a 'production' bath. How often do we take the time to have a really special bath? I believe that we need at least one big-production bath a week that is stage-managed for fun, relaxation and pleasure. Production baths can be full of bubbles or soothing essential oils. Like all wonderful productions, it helps to have them carefully lit and with

some well-chosen props. How about surrounding the bath with candles, crystals and flowers? Or perhaps having some soothing, sensual music playing in the background? For additional fun, add a special friend!

3) Have regular sessions with a massage therapist, a reflexologist, an aromatherapist, a hands-on healer or a beautician. Healing therapies and regular pampering are a necessary antidote to the stresses of modern living. If you do not have the money for regular sessions then team up with a friend, family member or lover to swap massages or pampering. You could even learn different healing skills and teach each other the basics.

4) Go for a walk. Pick your surroundings with care. The most beautiful, tranquil environments will have their own healing influence on you. The exercise of walking supports many of the body's natural functions and, if taken regularly, will raise energy levels.

5) Breathe deeply and monitor your breath. Your breath is a powerful key to your health and well-being. Consciously slowing down and deepening your breathing can improve the quality of your life and even extend it. If you find your breathing becoming shallow, take five or ten minutes to do something about it. You could place one hand on your stomach and one hand on your chest to make sure that you are filling and emptying your lungs properly. Then, breathe in to a count of eight and breathe out to a count of eight, ten, twelve or even more, consciously slowing down the out-breath.

6) Take ten-minute cat naps. Short bursts of sleep or meditation taken during the day can give your body some time to re-charge and re-balance itself. If you are out at work

during the day, ten minutes of complete rest during your lunch break when you are not eating, talking or shopping can make a significant difference to your stress levels, tolerance and performance. If you work from home, it may benefit you to start working a little earlier in the morning and have a couple of cat naps during the afternoon when your energy levels are lower.

7) Use your voice. Our voices have their own healing power. When we sing, yawn loudly, hum or chant, we liberate our feelings, discharge tensions and bathe our bodies with the healing vibration of our own unique sound. Do not let anyone convince you that you cannot sing, find your voice. It does not have to sound pretty to anyone else, it just needs to be used for your own pleasure and well-being. You could sing your positive affirmations to yourself!

8) Drink plenty of clean, fresh water and eat fresh raw vegetables. Our bodies are mainly made up of water, so it makes sense to replenish that water and have fluid passing through us that can help our bodies to clean away toxins. One of the many benefits of eating plenty of fresh raw vegetables and fruit as part of a balanced diet is that they have a high water content. The water has not been extracted by cooking and processing. Drinking plenty of water flushes the kidneys and helps them to function efficiently. However, it is preferable to drink when you are not eating a meal. Lots of liquid at meal-times could inhibit effective digestion of food.

9) Dance, stretch and move. Forget anything that you may have learned about dancing, let go of any judgements that you have and give your body the joy of spontaneous movement. Even if you can only move a small area of your

body, you can dance with it. Start with gentle stretching and then, with or without music, allow your body to find its own special way of moving. Dancing is life, to move is to live!

10) Stop when you are tired. This may seem easier said than done, particularly if you have a family to look after, a full-time job plus numerous additional commitments and responsibilities. When we allow ourselves to become over-tired, our bodies are often given more to contend with than just exhaustion. Rather than resting, we often over-eat, smoke more or drink more alcohol to compensate for the need that we are ignoring. Remind yourself that by stopping when you are tired today you are creating greater health and energy tomorrow to complete tasks comfortably and efficiently.

I am sure that you can find many more ways to direct love, care and attention to your body. This is just the beginning of a wonderful new relationship that you can create with yourself!

LEARNING TO LISTEN TO YOUR BODY

In choosing the appropriate diet, exercise programme, treatments and remedies it helps to learn to listen to your body. Listening to the messages that our bodies are giving us takes practice because we have actively learned lifestyles, beliefs and patterns of behaviour that block those messages and keep us in ignorance. Those messages may seem subtle and intangible in comparison to the information that we process in our brains, but they are still powerful and can tell us a lot about our health and well-being.

When we are actively listening to our bodies, we are more

able to pick up the early clues to areas of imbalance or disharmony. Acting on that information we can adjust our behaviour
or our lifestyle to help prevent illness or greater problems from
occurring. A simple example of this is listening to and acknowledging our tiredness and taking a rest when our bodies want to
and not when we have overdrawn on our physical reserves.

Another set of messages that we have learned to ignore are
those that come from our stomachs. Some of us carry on working all day without food despite the fact that our stomachs are
telling us to eat. Many more of us eat and continue to eat when
we are not hungry, ignoring signals that we are full, bloated or
even nauseated. In some cases we eat out of habit, in others we
eat for emotional reasons, stuffing down feelings of fear, anger,
joy and passion rather than acknowledging them. Linked with
this, we often eat because we are looking for some form of
instant gratification.

When we listen to our bodies we can also learn to detect the
underlying emotional, mental or spiritual causes of physical
problems. Physical pain, for example, may be telling us that
there is something physically wrong but it may also be telling
us that we have some unexpressed emotional pain that we
need to acknowledge and address.

The intelligence of the body is quite extraordinary. Our bodies hold memories of everything that has ever happened to us.
They retain the joyful memories and the painful ones, they
remember the feelings and the actions, the experiences and the
effects of those experiences; they hold an imprint that is not dis-
similar to a three-dimensional photograph. One way that we
can work with the intelligence of the body, to listen to its messages and to heal the mental, emotional and spiritual imprints
from the past, is to enter the body-mind.

As this is quite a detailed visualization, it may help you to read it through a few times before commencing. Alternatively, make a recording of yourself talking through the exercise slowly and play it back so that you can be your own healer and guide as you connect to your body's natural wisdom.

Find somewhere quiet and comfortable to sit, unplug the telephone and make sure that you are not going to be disturbed. Sit with your back supported, your body open and relaxed with your arms and legs uncrossed. If you prefer you can lie down for this, but again make sure that you keep your body open rather than curled up.

Place one hand gently on top of your stomach and just feel the rise and fall of your abdomen as you breathe. Consciously ask your body to breathe deeply and make sure that you are breathing all the way down to the bottom of your lungs. Allow your breath to become slower and be aware of keeping it full and deep without pushing or forcing it in, or out, of your lungs.

Still breathing deeply, take your attention to your head and imagine yourself residing within your mind, where you do your conscious thinking and reasoning. You could imagine this to be a creative and exciting place with lots of thoughts whizzing around at great speed like colourful flashes of electrical light. Knowing that you can safely return here when you need to, take your attention away from your head and back into your breath and your body.

Take a few moments to notice the sensations and feelings in your body. Are you tense? Are you relaxed? Are you comfortable? Is any part of you in pain? Is your body energized or is it tired? Just notice, without judgement, before bringing your attention to bear on your abdomen and imagining that within the centre of your gut is the 'mind of your body', the centre of your physical intelligence.

Imagine yourself entering your body-mind, knowing that it is safe for you to be there. In this part of you reside all of the clues to your physical health and well-being, all of the messages of how to stay in balance, all of the physical and emotional memories and all of the healing solutions. Within your body-mind there is a part of you that is always healthy, always in balance, always wise. As you breathe you access and expand that part of yourself, expanding and strengthening your awareness of what makes you healthy, happy and energized.

What does your body-mind look like? It might appear as a beautiful garden, a magnificent palace or a deep, blue ocean. If it is a garden, look for any areas that need tidying up, clearing or replanting, and picture this work going ahead. If it is a palace there may be some rooms that need renovating or cleaning – picture this taking place. A deep, blue ocean may also need cleaning (to remove environmental waste) and re-stocking with colourful fish and lush plant life. Whatever your image of your body-mind, see it becoming cleaner, brighter, stronger and more beautiful.

Imagine that by taking time to breathe deeply and to place your attention into your body you are releasing powerful but gentle forces of healing that are always available to you from within. Every breath connects you more and more to your self-healing power and increases your awareness of what your body needs to keep itself healthy, active, energized and comfortable. Ask your body for any information that would benefit you at this time. What could you be doing to support your health and well-being? Notice any ideas, feelings and responses that you have.

You can take anything up to an hour or more to do this exercise, but it would be better to take five or ten minutes to do it regularly than spend longer and only do it once. The advantage of a longer body-mind visualization is that it may facilitate a powerful process of healing and bring you some interesting information that you may not get in five minutes. The advantage of doing lots of shorter ones is that you will strengthen your connection between your intellect and your physical awareness.

When you complete the process, take a couple of minutes to place your attention back into your head and see it filled with wonderful, creative, positive thoughts. Write down or record any insights that you get. If during this visualization you have had an impulse to start a new exercise programme or find out about treatments or take greater care of your diet, then remember to act on these impulses as soon as you can.

Exercise: Learning to Listen to your Body-Mind
Whenever you have a particular physical need or problem you
can go to your body-mind and ask for information.

Physical Problems

With any physical problem from a headache to a sprained ankle
or from a cancerous growth to a condition of depleted immunity you can go to your body-mind and ask for information
about the underlying cause of the problem and gain insights for
treatments, solutions and the management of symptoms.

Using the above visualization, take your awareness into your
body-mind and then focus upon the area of your body that is
damaged, sick or uncomfortable. If you are dealing with a general condition such as one of depleted immunity, focus upon
your whole body. Deepen your breathing and imagine that
your breath moves beyond your lungs into the area or areas
that need healing, filling them with energy, peace and new life.

Almost as if you were able to switch on listening devices or
amplifiers inside your body, imagine that you can listen to
what is going on. The information may come to you in the form
of feelings, impressions, thoughts, images, sensations or inner
voices. Just notice and make a note of any ideas, insights or
impressions that you receive once you have completed the
exercise. It may help you to ask your body some appropriate
questions. Here are some ideas to help.

*What is the underlying cause of this problem/condition/illness/
pain/restriction/symptom?* (Choose whatever is appropriate
for you.)

*What can I do to heal my arm/digestion/breast/lungs/immune
system/back, etc.?*

How can I release or heal the pain/discomfort/blockage/restric-tion/disease?

How can I best manage or transform my symptoms?

Is this problem/condition caused by unexpressed emotion/poor diet/negative or limiting beliefs/bad posture/lack of exercise/fear, etc.?

What do I need to be doing differently in my life in order to heal myself?

Listening to physical information and asking for guidance takes practice. Do not feel put off if you do not receive direct answers to your questions. Sometimes it is enough to ask for information and be willing to listen to your body for a process of healing to begin.

Diet and Exercise

You can ask your body-mind about the suitability of any foods, exercise or treatments before and after you take them. Various therapists test the body's responses to a treatment before rec-ommending it to their patients. Kinesiologists do something called 'muscle testing', for example, which is a system of ask-ing the body for direct information about healing, food toler-ance or therapies and gaining an immediate physical reaction. Some other therapists use equipment to measure changes in the body's subtle electricity in response to a wide range of sub-stances or enquiries.

For yourself, prepare a list of questions to ask your body-mind, or put together a collection of foods, medications and remedies to test with your body-mind. Have everything with-in easy reach, then either ask yourself the appropriate question, such as:

What foods would it benefit me to eat at this time?

What foods are best avoided at this time?

How can I best exercise my body?

What kind of treatment do I need for this condition?

or hold one substance at a time on the top of your chest (at your breast bone) and ask your body whether it is right for you. Would it be beneficial for your body or harmful? Allow plenty of time for a response before moving on to the next question or substance.

One of the questions that you can ask your body is *'Will this raise my energy or lower it? Will this energize me or deplete me?'* Having asked the question and acted upon your 'gut response', you can check out whether you were right simply by noticing what happens to your energy levels after you have put your insights into action. Making a healthy choice generally brings about an increase in energy.

Please do not use this exercise as a substitute for appropriate medical and complementary health care. As well as helping you to prevent illness and heal yourself, the information that you receive can help you to make wise choices when you are following professional advice or undergoing treatment. This information can also support the effectiveness of your chosen treatments, but it cannot replace them. The most important thing is to work with the intelligence of your body as much as you can rather than working against it.

THE WISDOM
OF YOUR EMOTIONS

THE POWER OF YOUR EMOTIONS

Just as your body has its own intelligence, so have your emotions. Our emotions are a constant source of energy, creativity and personal power that can be tapped for self-healing. They have their own wisdom, rhythm and timing which, given the right conditions, can help to keep us healthy. It is our feelings that bring colour into our lives. We are motivated by our passions or our anger, lifted by our joy, deepened by our sadness and inspired by our capacity to love.

It is the misuse, misdirection and suppression of our emotional energy that contributes to many illnesses and relationship problems. We have learned to choke back some of our feelings and distort others with our negative or limiting beliefs so that they either become overly controlled or out of control. Emotions that are not expressed or that become over-emphasized can create a physical imbalance and affect our ability to communicate our true needs and desires.

As we grow up, we learn not only a vast vocabulary of thoughts and beliefs but also about the expression of emotions. In most cases, babies are emotionally straightforward. When they are happy, they gurgle with delight; when they are distressed or angry, they yell and scream. Their communication is essentially simple, direct and effective. They give clear signals to their parents or parent figures whenever they are content or uncomfortable, hungry or in need of attention. It is only as they grow and develop that their emotional lives become more complex.

As children, we copy the emotional behaviour that we observe around us. If our parents are good at expressing anger but not very good at expressing love or sadness it is likely that we will develop similar emotional patterns. If our parents approve of us when we are all smiles but ignore us when we are tearful or angry then we will learn to wear a smile regardless of our underlying feelings. We could be boiling with rage but still smile because to do otherwise would risk disapproval.

Our vocabulary of beliefs and our patterns of emotional behaviour are often inextricably linked. We pick up direct judgements about our emotions and we learn to think about our feelings in ways that inhibit them, deny them or over-emphasize them. This is how we create the conflict between the head, the heart and the voice that I talked about in Chapter 1. We have feelings and desires but our beliefs do not give us permission to have them and so our expression becomes suppressed or distorted.

For example, as children we may have demonstrated a high level of joy and passion that was considered to be unacceptable. We may have been naturally enthusiastic people whose parents were not in touch with their own enthusiasm and excitement and who therefore had a problem handling ours. Children can become passionately joyful about anything from a beautiful flower to a wonderful new toy and from a new way of playing a game to a visit from Grandma. Perhaps that enthusiasm needs safe boundaries so that it does not become entirely disruptive or inappropriate to the situation, but it also needs to be encouraged, accepted and approved of so that it can contribute to a lifetime of safe, joyful pleasure.

Parents who were not given permission to be joyful and passionate when they were children do not always know how to give their own children that permission. Parents who were not taught how to accept their anger and express it safely are often unable to pass these skills on to their children. People whose own parents were not very permissive and accepting of their sadness, disappointment, distress or grief do not necessarily have the experience to permit these feelings in their children, unless they have learned to break free of their conditioning and liberate themselves from their families' emotional patterns.

In some cases, the beliefs and patterns of behaviour that we learn leave us unable to recognize many of our feelings. As children, when we become angry or too demanding we are often told that we are tired. Sometimes this is true and sometimes not, it is just easier to label demanding behaviour as tiredness than acknowledge the needs or feelings that are present. As adults, we may not think of ourselves as being particularly emotional but every time we become angry or have needs to be addressed we may find ourselves becoming sleepy. We have learned that it is safer to become unconscious than to address our emotions.

Sometimes it is valuable to look back to childhood and remind ourselves where some of our beliefs and emotional patterns came from. Looking back at the past can give us insights about the choices that we have made and help us to make new choices in our lives right now. It does not help to look back to the past with the intention to blame our parents, families, teachers or friends for the problems that we have had in our lives. Nor does it serve our process of self-healing to blame ourselves for past choices and mistakes. We simply need to look for information that will broaden our understanding, help us to leave the past behind and create something totally different in the present and the future.

Exercise: Mapping your Emotions

With a pen and paper make a list of the emotions that were expressed or not expressed when you were growing up. In addition, make a note of anything that was said to you about emotions. Here are some questions to help you:

What emotions were expressed to you or around you? Were your parents or parent figures comfortable about expressing sadness, anger, love, joy, excitement or fear? Did they cry, yell and laugh? What emotions did they express most often? Here are some examples to jog your memory:

> 'My father expressed a great deal of anger and passion when he was discussing politics but never cried in front of us, nor was he particularly joyful.'

> 'My mother would cry a lot, almost too much. She would cry rather than get angry or deal with a problem directly.'

> 'My father was very loving and sensitive at home but he had a public face that was quite different. When in company, we were all expected to have a stiff upper lip and not make a scene, just like Daddy.'

> 'My mother was always angry with me and rarely loving and tender. I was frightened of her anger and used to hide from her.'

What was said to you or around you about emotions? Were you given permission to express all of your feelings? Did you get strong messages from your parents, brothers, sisters, grandparents, teachers or peers about the emotions that were acceptable or unacceptable? Here are some examples:

'Boys do not cry.'

'You are too old to cry.'

'You've got to put a brave face on things.'

'Do not show them how you feel.'

'Girls shouldn't shout and be aggressive.'

'You sound funny when you laugh.'

'You look really ugly when you cry.'

What emotions are you comfortable expressing in your life now? Are you comfortable with other people's anger, sadness, joy, excitement, etc.? Are there some emotions that you fear having because you are scared of getting stuck in them or becoming out of control? Write down as much information as you can without judging or criticizing yourself.

Leave plenty of space to add any more information that comes to the surface of your mind during the next couple of days. Next, take a large, clean sheet of paper and draw a big circle upon it. Imagine that the circle represents your full emotional potential. If you were completely comfortable with all of your emotions and were able to express them fully, appropriately and safely you would be able to claim all of the space in the circle. If you were comfortable with most of your emotions, you would be able to claim most of the space. If you were comfortable with just a few areas of emotional expression, you would be able to claim just a small space in the circle.

With a pen or pencil, instinctively shade in as much of the circle as you are comfortable with. Leave areas to represent the emotions that you feel cut off from or that you would feel embarrassed to express. Also leave areas to represent the emotions that you feel unsafe with or that you fear will send you out of control if you were to express them. If it helps you to do this, you could write some of the emotions into the circle so that you may, for example, shade in the area that you have labelled 'sadness', leave blank the area that you have labelled 'anger' and half-shade the area labelled 'excitement'.

The information that you have recorded will begin a process of emotional change inside you and provide you with insights to help you take the next steps forward. It may help you to draw this circle of emotional potential on a regular basis so that you can monitor improvements in your emotional comfort and expression. The information in your list could provide you with the raw material for some new positive affirmations. Here are some affirmational ideas to start you off.

Affirmations for Healing your Emotions

- IT IS SAFE FOR ME TO BE IN TOUCH WITH MY FEELINGS.

- IT IS SAFE FOR ME TO EXPRESS ALL OF MY FEELINGS.

- I MAKE FRIENDS WITH MY EMOTIONS.

- IT IS SAFE FOR ME TO LOVE.

- MY EMOTIONS ARE ALWAYS IN BALANCE.

- I LIBERATE AND EXPRESS MY EMOTIONAL POWER.

TRANSFORMING THE MESSAGES FROM THE PAST

Here are some examples of how to turn old, parental messages into new, positive affirmations:

Examples:

- *'My father expressed a great deal of anger and passion when he was discussing politics but never cried in front of us, nor was he particularly joyful.'*

- *'My mother would cry a lot, almost too much. She would cry rather than get angry or deal with a problem directly.'*

Affirmations:

- IT IS SAFE FOR ME TO CRY.

- IT IS EASY FOR ME TO HANDLE MY ANGER.

- I HAVE A HEALTHY BALANCE OF ANGER, SADNESS, PASSION AND JOY.

- IT IS SAFE AND EASY FOR ME TO EXPRESS MY FEELINGS DIRECTLY.

Example:

- *'My father was very loving and sensitive at home but he had a public face that was quite different. When in company, we were all expected to have a stiff upper lip and not make a scene, just like Daddy.'*

Affirmations:

- IT IS SAFE FOR ME TO BE EMOTIONAL IN FRONT OF OTHER PEOPLE.

- MY LOVE AND SENSITIVITY SUPPORTS ME WHEREVER I GO.

Examples:

- *'You've got to put a brave face on things.'*
- *'Do not show them how you feel.'*

Affirmation:

- IT IS SAFE TO LET MY FEELINGS SHOW.

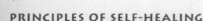

- *'Girls shouldn't shout and be aggressive.'*

Affirmation:

- I GIVE MYSELF PERMISSION TO BE A POWERFUL, PASSIONATE WOMAN.

Example:

- *'You look really ugly when you cry.'*

Affirmation:

- MY FEELINGS ARE BEAUTIFUL AND SO AM I.

Now turn your own negative messages from the past into positive affirmations for regular use.

Visualization: *Exploring your Emotional Potential*

Find somewhere quiet and comfortable to sit, unplug the telephone and make sure that you are not going to be disturbed. Sit with your back supported, your body open and relaxed with your arms and legs uncrossed. If you prefer you can lie down for this, but again make sure that you keep your body open rather than curled up.

Place one hand gently on the top of your stomach and just feel the rise and fall of your abdomen as you breathe. Breathe deeply and imagine that your breath is helping you to connect to your feelings, safely and effectively. Each breath gently stimulates and liberates trapped emotional energy inside you, dissolving the stresses and tensions of the past. If any feelings come straight to the surface just breathe in to them and allow them to be there. If not, just trust that there is some emotional healing taking place inside you.

Imagine that your emotions are a garden of beautiful flowers and picture yourself clearing away rubbish from that garden so that the flowers can grow and bloom without obstruction. In your mind, remove the litter of negative or limiting thoughts, pull up the choking weeds of old judgements and carefully water your emotions with loving acceptance. See them grow stronger, more colourful and more beautiful, lush and fragrant with creativity and self-healing power. As I write this, I think of full velvety roses, but use your own imagination to create the garden that you choose or even to create a totally different set of images. It is important that you make this meaningful for you.

Picture yourself safely and effectively expressing your emotions in all areas of your life, developing emotional honesty in all of your relationships and releasing emotional tension easily and with joy. In your mind, ask yourself, *'What do I need to express in my life right now?'* and *'What can I do to heal my emotions?'* Allow yourself the space to receive any insights, impressions and feelings that arise. You could also ask yourself, *'What emotional patterns are contributing to my illness/problem/disease?'*

When you complete this visualization, affirm to yourself a few times,

- I AM WILLING TO LIBERATE THE HEALING POWER OF MY EMOTIONS.

Write down or record any insights that you had during this exercise, and remember to act on them!

What do our illnesses say about our emotional state and our ability to express our feelings? Certainly, a person's emotional state needs to be considered in all areas of healing; if there is illness or imbalance then there is generally an emotional factor that needs to be acknowledged and addressed. In some cases the emotions are major contributors to the condition or the problem, in other cases they are not a significant part of the initial cause but they become significant once the first symptoms have been established.

Illness can be said to be an expression of an inner conflict. When there is an underlying mental, emotional or spiritual tension that affects our well-being, we seek to express, resolve and release that tension in the best way that we know how. If we have not learned to do it in any other way, we do it by creating symptoms. A symptom is a signal that there is some underlying imbalance; it is an indication to ourselves and to others that we need some care and attention. It is rare for the cause of that imbalance to be purely physical.

EMOTION AND INJURY

We often consider our injuries to be purely physical. We cut our finger, break a leg or damage our spine in an accident and we can clearly pinpoint a physical reason for our problem. However, our mental and emotional state could also have contributed to our initial injury and could well be contributing to the rate of our recovery and our ability to manage our symptoms.

The timing of an injury is often significant, and it is always useful to ask yourself what was going on in your life at the time when you injured yourself. What was happening around you and what were your underlying thoughts and feelings? The timing of your recovery is also significant. What is happening around you and inside you as your pain diminishes or your body repairs itself?

RALPH'S STORY

Ralph was a kind and honourable man in his mid-sixties who came to me for some hands-on healing and guided relaxation after he had injured his back. Ralph was very emotional but, like many men, particularly older men, he was unable to recognize and acknowledge many of his emotions. He had always been an excellent provider for his wife and family, fulfilling a traditional male role with a great deal of love and commitment even though it had not always been easy for him. As he had anticipated, his children had grown up and moved away and he and his wife had continued to live in the family home, a three-bedroom house on which they had a long-term mortgage. On approaching retirement Ralph made various investments that he calculated would help them to meet the regular monthly repayments on the house and supplement their pensions.

For a while, all went well. Ralph and his wife were able to pay the bills, keep up the house and have a little left over to provide for some luxuries and a little back-up support for their children. Then they experienced some unexpected changes. A couple of Ralph's investments failed rather dramatically, reducing their projected income, and then interest rates fell, affecting the income from their 'safer' investments. In addition, they discovered some repairs that needed doing to the roof of their house – in short, the figures did not add up any more. Their only solution was to put their house on the market and hope for the best.

Ralph felt guilty that he had made some bad investments and felt sad and distressed that he and his wife had to leave the family home. He felt that he had failed his wife and family, but decided that he had to put a brave face on things for their sake and found a buyer for the house quite quickly. They found a smaller house that they could afford and made preparations to move. It was then that Ralph injured his back.

Ralph was packing up some china and reached down to pick up a vase. His back locked into position and he suffered intense spasms of pain. During the entire process of the move, Ralph was flat on his back recovering and his family took over the details of packing, transporting and unpacking their belongings. When Ralph visited me, he was getting better after having received medical attention and some physical manipulation, but he was still in a great deal of pain and he was still very upset.

Ralph began to talk through his experiences and started to acknowledge some of his feelings for the first time. He had many judgements about having to remain strong, put a brave face on things and cope with his situation; this inability to express his feelings had added greatly to the stress of the move. He was giving himself a hard time about what had happened, blaming himself for the choices that he had made and punishing himself with guilt.

I helped Ralph to let go of some of his judgements and encouraged him to stop punishing himself. I also told him that to continue to heal his back and let go of the physical pain, he needed to acknowledge and express the emotional pain that he felt. By the end of the first session, Ralph was feeling better. By the third session he was able to talk more openly about his feelings and he even shed a few tears. Afterwards, his pain lifted and he breathed a sigh of relief. I gave him some affirmations to help him adapt to his new life and let go of the past, which included:

- **I AM WILLING TO FORGIVE MYSELF.**

- **I ALLOW MYSELF TO EXPRESS ALL OF MY FEELINGS.**

- **I GIVE MYSELF PERMISSION TO ASK FOR HELP WHEN I NEED IT.**

- I TRUST MYSELF TO CREATE WONDERFUL NEW EXPERIENCES IN MY LIFE.

- I AM PHYSICALLY AND EMOTIONALLY HEALTHY.

- I AM ALWAYS SUPPORTED IN MAKING THE RIGHT CHOICES.

I continued to see Ralph as he adjusted to the changes in his circumstances and came to terms with more of his suppressed feelings. Within a short time, he and his wife discovered that they were much happier in their new home. They were closer to some of their friends and it was easier to look after than their previous house had been. Although it took a little time to reorganize their finances, they felt a greater and greater sense of freedom as they realized that their financial commitments had significantly reduced. After a while, some of Ralph's more successful investments began to pay off and they were able to have some holidays that they may not have been able to afford if they had stayed in their previous home.

EMOTION AND DISEASE

The diseases and infections that we create in our bodies all have their mental and emotional factors. It is always valid to ask yourself, *'What are the beliefs and emotions that are contributing to this condition?'*, *'What changes of belief will help me to heal this?'* and *'What emotions do I need to acknowledge and express in order to help me heal myself?'*

When we are sick, the first emotional clues that we have are the feelings that go hand in hand with our symptoms. We can ask ourselves, *'How does this illness make me feel?'* If your cold makes you feel sad then it is valid to assume that some previously unexpressed sadness has contributed to the creation of your condition. Colds are often a way that we detoxify ourselves. They help to clear our bodies of accumulated junk and our emotional selves of unexpressed feelings. They also help to

If you have a cold, trust the feelings that you have and work with them rather than denying them.

Similarly, if we develop a more extreme condition, such as a form of cancer, it is important that we work with our thoughts and feelings. If our response to our diagnosis is shock, anger and grief then it would be worth exploring these feelings further, as they may have contributed to the creation of the condition and may well contribute to some healing solutions. A willingness to acknowledge our emotions could powerfully support the effectiveness of our chosen treatments and help to prevent a reoccurrence of the disease. From my experience, many forms of cancer are related to some powerful, unexpressed feelings, particularly anger.

Our emotions do have their own wisdom. When we trust them and give ourselves permission to have them then they help us to heal. Emotions are creative energy; when we acknowledge them, express them and release them they can help us to create wonderful experiences in our lives, bringing colour to our relationships and motivation to our spiritual purpose. When we deny them, hold on to them or build them up out of all proportion with negative or fearful thoughts then we risk turning that creative energy back on itself, and that is when they contribute to disease and disharmony.

EMOTION AND LONG-TERM ILLNESS

With long-term illness it becomes even more essential to remain emotionally open and fluid. The prevention of further deterioration and the successful management of symptoms are greatly helped by the ongoing management and healing of emotions. When, for instance, we have weak spots in our bodies from old injuries or debilitating disease we may experience a level of physical pain that is directly related to the condition

itself, although the extent of the pain that we feel may be greatly increased by mental and emotional factors. Unexpressed
emotional pain is often felt as additional physical pain, as are
mental patterns of self-punishment, self-criticism and guilt.
Simply put, our unresolved issues and unexpressed feelings
have a tendency to settle in our physical weak spots.

I believe that painkilling drugs are a miracle of the modern
age that allow many people to live with dignity and in relative
comfort. However, I also believe that they are often over-used.
Pain is a warning that there is something wrong, it indicates
that there is something that we need to change or resolve.
Listening to the pain and working with it can help us to make
the physical, mental and emotional changes necessary to heal
the cause of the pain or at least diminish it. When we knock out
the pain with drugs we may detach ourselves from the underlying cause of the pain and therefore cut ourselves off from
potential healing solutions.

With long-term illnesses that bring continual pain, we need
to make the appropriate choices about effective pain management but we also need to listen to ourselves so that we are continuing to address any underlying emotional and psychological
issues. This may mean getting appropriate medical advice
about reducing painkillers and supplementing with relaxation
techniques, regular sessions with a spiritual or hands-on healer, counselling or complementary therapies. Let us manage our
pain without deadening our self-healing power.

One of the most effective ways to stimulate a process of
emotional healing is to bring acceptance and forgiveness to our
illness or problem. It may seem a strange idea to 'forgive' your
disease or 'learn to love' your condition, but our illnesses and
problems represent a part of ourselves that needs our acceptance in order to heal. The energy used in hating or despising
our condition has a tendency to keep us attached to it, whereas

Exercise: Forgiving your Illness

With pen and paper, write a list of your conditions, symptoms and problems. This could include areas of disease, injury or imbalance in your body, confusion or negativity in your mind, or emotional imbalances such as depression, jealousy or extreme fear. Here are some examples to help you (not meant to be a comprehensive list of symptoms or effects, just a starting point for your own thoughts):

CONDITION	SYMPTOMS
Arthritis	Painful joints, lack of mobility
Stomach ulcers	Stomach pain, indigestion
Migraines	Nausea, headaches, sensitivity to light
Depression	Lack of motivation, numbness, fatigue, an absence of feelings
Violent anger	Going out of control, saying or doing things that are destructive to friendships and family relationships, periods of extreme guilt or remorse
Repeating patterns of self-criticism	Lack of self-worth, guilt, pain and self-punishment

Then, write a series of positive declarations for everything on your list, using the following suggestions as a starting point:

- I FORGIVE MY ... (condition).

- I FORGIVE MYSELF FOR HAVING/BEING ... (symptoms or effects).

- I LOVINGLY RELEASE MY ... (condition, symptoms or effects).

- I NOW CREATE NEW HEALING SOLUTIONS.

Here are some examples:

- I FORGIVE MY ARTHRITIS.

- I FORGIVE MYSELF FOR HAVING PAINFUL JOINTS AND A LACK OF MOBILITY.

- I LOVINGLY RELEASE MY ARTHRITIS, PAINFUL JOINTS AND LACK OF MOBILITY.

- I NOW CREATE NEW HEALING SOLUTIONS.

- I FORGIVE MY DEPRESSION.

- I FORGIVE MYSELF FOR BEING UNMOTIVATED AND FOR FEELING NUMB.

- I LOVINGLY RELEASE MY DEPRESSION, LACK OF MOTIVA- TION AND NUMBNESS.

- I NOW CREATE NEW HEALING SOLUTIONS.

The first three declarations are not for regular use. Unlike the affirmations that we have practised, they are a one-off state- ment or occasional declaration of forgiveness and release. The reason for this is that they would keep our minds unduly focused upon the condition or symptoms that we wish to release if repeated over and over again. The fourth declaration can be used as an affirmation because it is focused upon some- thing positive that we wish to create.

Read your declarations through a couple of times, ideally out loud, so that you hear the sound of your own voice. Even better, take them to a mirror and declare them to yourself once or twice over as you look at your reflection. Remember to say them slowly and clearly and make sure that you breathe full, deep breaths as you do so. Then follow up with some general affirmations of health, well-being and forgiveness that are not focused on your condition. Here are some ideas:

- I FORGIVE MYSELF COMPLETELY.

- I AM WILLING TO FORGIVE MYSELF AND SET MYSELF FREE.

- I GIVE MYSELF PERMISSION TO HEAL.

- I LOVE EVERY PART OF MYSELF.

- I AM MAGNETIC TO THE TREATMENTS, HELP AND SUPPORT THAT I NEED.

and once again,

- I NOW CREATE NEW HEALING SOLUTIONS.

If your declarations or affirmations touch any feelings and bring some underlying areas of anger, resentment, joy, fear, excitement or pain to the surface, then allow them to be there. Emotional changes are part of the process of healing; it may just feel a little odd when some emotions first begin to emerge. Breathe into them, do your best to accept them, give yourself some reassurance and remember to use some affirmations of emotional safety.

Learning to acknowledge and express our emotions takes practice, particularly if we have been cut off from some of them for a long time, so it is important that we are patient and gentle with ourselves. Here are some ideas to help.

1) Declare your feelings as soon as you notice them. One mistake we often make is that we consider our emotions to be too insignificant to be worth mentioning. We often just bite our lips and carry on, building up reservoirs of unexpressed sadness or resentment in the process. If, instead, we simply say, *'I am sad about this'* or *'Please stop doing that, it makes me angry'* we are able to discharge and resolve our feelings harmlessly rather than allow them to build until they become disproportionate to our original reaction or grievance.

   If you do not feel able to declare your feelings to somebody else at the very least declare them to yourself! It is healthy to feel, express and let go of your feelings; it is unhealthy to deny, swallow and hold on to them.

2) Role play your feelings. If you have something that you need to express to another person and he or she is either unavailable or unable to listen to you, you can role-play a conversation instead. Find somewhere quiet where you will not be disturbed, and sit comfortably. Visualize or imagine the person that you need to talk to sitting in front of you and then begin to speak your mind. Explain how you are feeling. If you are angry say *'I am angry'* and explain why. If you are sad, say so and give reasons. If you need to say that you love this person, say it a few times until you get a stronger feeling of what you are saying. It is fine to repeat yourself, it will help you to connect to your feelings and clear them.

   When you have finished, envision this person surrounded with the light of healing, then imagine the image dissolving harmlessly away. In your mind, place healing light around yourself too and talk to yourself using words of encouragement and reassurance. You could say,

- I AM SAFE.

- I AM SAFE WITH MY FEELINGS.

- I TRUST MY INNER WISDOM.

- Write down what you feel, or talk into a tape recorder. It is important to get your thoughts and feelings out rather than have them building inside you. Writing or recording them may help. Sometimes it is valuable to keep what you have written or taped, and sometimes the act of ripping up your notes or wiping the tape can be symbolically healing in itself. You decide what is appropriate. Remember that your notes may be a good source of ideas to help you create some new positive affirmations.

- Go for counselling or therapy. Not all forms of analytical or psychological therapies are appropriate for everyone and they may not be helpful if we become dependent upon them long term, but they can help to facilitate wonderful breakthroughs and stimulate emotional healing. Straightforward counselling with a sensitive and experienced listener is always a good idea. It helps us to clarify our thoughts, make sense of our experiences and make new positive choices. In addition, the process of talking things through can powerfully connect us to our underlying feelings.

- Give yourself some moments of stillness and silence. We spend so much of our lives rushing around that we do not always leave space to listen to and notice our emotions. Some of us even create activity and noise in our lives precisely so we can avoid our underlying feelings. Regularly giving yourself the gift of stillness and silence will help you to stay in touch with your inner needs and drives.

- Find safe ways to channel your anger. Anger is often dispelled through safe, physical activity. Punch pillows, take vigorous exercise or have a good yell. Just make sure that the activities you choose are appropriate for your physical capabilities and that they are truly safe for yourself and for the people around you.

- Notice and adjust your compulsive behaviour. What do you do to suppress your emotions? Some of us eat too much, some of us drink alcohol and some of us smoke. Some of us may have other forms of compulsive behaviour such as cleaning obsessively or becoming overly concerned with minor details. The things that we do compulsively could be a cover for unexpressed emotional needs, desires and conflicts.

   It is sometimes valuable to take a few minutes before we eat, drink or light up to ask ourselves, *'What is the underlying need?'*, *'What am I feeling right now?'* and *'How can I best take care of myself now?'* Addressing these needs and feelings takes away the impulse to behave compulsively. For some forms of compulsive behaviour we may need to seek the help of a doctor, a counsellor or a healer. Self-help groups such as Alcoholics Anonymous, Narcotics Anonymous and Over-eaters Anonymous may also provide an important source of support.

- Allow yourself to be moved and inspired. What moves you? What inspires you to be passionate or to take action? Anything from old romantic movies to a beautiful piece of music can stimulate safe emotional release. When we discover the things that move us, we can learn to use them constructively to keep us connected to our feelings and desires.

- Learn to notice how you switch your feelings off and choose to switch them back on again. Most of us have developed defence mechanisms that deflect potentially emotional situations. For some of us, we use patterns of cynical thought and behaviour to stop us from acknowledging our true feelings. While it is important to question things and weigh up their value with careful consideration, denying ourselves experiences, relationships or intimacy because of our learned cynical responses is self-defeating. Cynicism is fear-based, it robs us of energy, limits our opportunities and inhibits the natural, healthy process of life.

  Some of us have become very clever at using humour as a defence. Perhaps when we were children we learned that making our parents, our teachers or other children laugh was a good way of keeping ourselves safe and diffusing emotionally charged situations. As adults, we crack jokes when we are hurting or when others tells us that they love us or when we do not want to admit that someone is angry with us or that we are angry with them. Some of us laugh when we really want to cry, and this is not always healthy. Humour and laughter are powerful tools for self-healing except when they are used to cover up our feelings. We need to be willing to listen to our feelings, notice our automatic responses, choose to behave or think differently and adapt to handling rather than denying our feelings. Like many things of value, this takes practice.

- Be willing to become more intimate and honest with other people. One way that we switch our feelings off and deny them is by withdrawing from potentially emotional situations. I have known people who break up relationships rather than allow themselves to get closer to their friends or lovers. Getting closer to someone challenges us to acknowledge and accept more of our underlying feelings.

If we have learned, in childhood, that some of our feelings are unlovable, then we are often scared of allowing them to become visible. The reality of getting closer to other people is that we inevitably become more 'visible' to them and, in so doing, we become more visible to ourselves. When we are willing to change our beliefs, become more emotionally honest with ourselves and risk intimacy with others, the experience that we create is quite different from our previous fears and expectations. When we love and accept them, our emotions are wonderful!

LIVING IN THE PRESENT

A POSITION OF POWER

One of the most exciting things that I have learned from my own personal development and from helping other people to heal and transform their lives is that we all have the power to change for the better. Regardless of our situation, our state of health or our background there is always something that we can do to heal and improve our lives. We just need to discover that we have that power and learn how to exercise it.

It does not matter what we have done in the past, what mistakes we have made, what we have suffered or how we have been hurt; we can make new choices in this present moment that allow our lives to be different. Many people carry around guilt about something that they did or said in the past, a missed opportunity or a choice that did not work out, and expect their lives to be continually marred because of it. They feel that happiness or well-being is undeserved and unobtainable because of some past mistake or twist of fate. Many more of us develop a belief that life is always going to be the same way. We assume, for example, that because our last three relationships failed the next one is bound to be a failure, too. It really does not need to be like that. We have a choice.

We need to be willing to make the changes within ourselves that allow our lives to change for the better. When we replace our negative beliefs with positive ones, trade our old emotional patterns for new healthy ones and care for our bodies, we make ourselves available for a very different experience of life. The past is complete, it has taught us many things but we do not have to be forever bound by what we have learned, particularly if our beliefs and behaviour no longer serve us in health and happiness. Each new moment provides us with the opportunity to create our lives anew. We are all in a position of power.

PAST, PRESENT AND FUTURE

We often avoid the present moment. We spend so much time dwelling on the past and what might have been or fantasizing about the future and either hoping for the best or dreading the worst that we sometimes forget the gift of what is currently available to us. The present moment can seem too scary to contemplate, it is filled with so many possibilities for healing, so many solutions and so many feelings that we have learned to suppress that we look for any distraction. The present moment is powerful, it requires us to be responsible for ourselves, responsible for the choices that we are making and honest about our needs, desires and feelings.

To live in the present does not mean giving up our memories of the past or our dreams of the future, rather it means that we need to put all of that into perspective as we get on with our lives and make the best choices we know how to make at this present time. There is a big difference between looking at the past to heal it, forgive it, learn from it and move on and looking at the past in order to wallow in it, get stuck in it and allow it to get in the way of what we are creating in our lives now. There is also a big difference between focusing positively upon what we wish to create in the future and fantasizing about the future to the exclusion of taking care of ourselves now. It is fine to have our heads stuck in the clouds as long as we have our feet firmly on the ground at the same time.

Looking back at the past has value because doing so can help us to make sense of our lives and clear any unresolved issues that we are allowing to impede our current happiness. Planning for the future is important because our dreams and desires help to create a positive forward direction that strongly influences the choices we make. However, the present moment is the one that offers us the greatest opportunities for transformation. It is *now* that we can have the greatest impact on our health, happiness and well-being. We need to listen now, notice now, choose now, adapt now and act now in order to alter the course of our lives for the better.

Visualization: Living in the Present

Find somewhere quiet and comfortable to sit, unplug the telephone and make sure that you are not going to be disturbed. Sit with your back supported, your body open and relaxed with your arms and legs uncrossed. If you prefer you can lie down for this, but again make sure that you keep your body open rather than curled up.

Breathe deeply and take your attention into your body and into your emotions. How and what are you feeling right now? Just notice, without judgement. Imagine that the cells of your body contain a memory of everything that has ever happened to you. It is as if they have been programmed like a computer to respond to all of your past experiences and all of the choices that you made about yourself as you were growing up. To some extent they are still responding to these past choices now, even if these choices bear no relevance to your present happiness and your future potential.

As you continue to breathe long, slow, deep breaths, picture every cell of your body filling with bright, golden, healing light. The light heals and dissolves the impact of any past experiences that do not support you in creating health and happiness in your life right now. This healing energy releases you from all old fears, guilt and pain, dissolving old negative thoughts and making you available for new positive experiences. Imagine your body, mind and emotions being born anew; picture yourself being created to live fully in the present moment, programmed for health, joy, fulfilment and success.

See yourself living fully in the present, creating the relationships, feelings and experiences that give you the greatest pleasure, constantly recreating yourself in health and happiness. Imagine yourself with a new freedom that allows you to do whatever best serves you without restriction. You are no longer inhibited by any negative choices or experiences from the past. What do you do differently? What new choices would you like to make? What is the most positive, healing thing that you can do for yourself right now?

When you have completed this visualization, make a note of any insights that you had and remember to seize the opportunity of the present moment and act upon them.

RESPONSIBILITY AND BLAME

One reason that we sometimes fear or avoid the power of the present moment is that it invites us to take responsibility for our lives. As children we often learn that responsibility is a dangerous thing. Many of us have great confusion in our minds concerning the difference between responsibility and blame. When parents or teachers told us that we were responsible for something it often meant that we would be criticized or blamed if we made a mistake. As adults we become reluctant to take risks and, rather than seize the moment, we wait for someone else to give us permission to do things or hope that someone else is going to do them instead of us. Then we too look for someone to blame if it all goes wrong.

Generation by generation we perpetuate beliefs in failure. We often expect life to fail us and we often expect to fail ourselves. We even have expressions that back up our beliefs, such as, *'Don't stick your neck out, you will get it chopped off!'* Those of us who are highly successful spiritually, emotionally or materially are often those who have learned to feel comfortable with responsibility and who have been willing to go beyond their limiting expectations and develop a strong belief in success. They expect to be rewarded rather than blamed.

Responsibility is personal power; blame is impotence. If we realize that we are responsible for our health we can take steps to improve it, manage it and prevent illness from occurring. We can take positive risks to keep ourselves healthy, such as to risk asking for the help that we need, risk leaving a job that distresses us in favour of one that brings us fulfilment, risk being honest about our feelings or risk doing something new. In taking responsibility for our well-being and happiness and expecting success we invite it and we begin living our lives with a positive, self-fulfilling prophecy.

When we blame, we disempower ourselves. We perpetuate patterns of belief and behaviour that we learn from other people and continue to restrict or punish ourselves with our thoughts. Blaming other people keeps us stuck, it is a way that we rob ourselves of the power to change our situation for the better. For example, we often blame our marriage partner or lover for not being able to anticipate and fulfil all of our needs. This pattern of thought and behaviour inhibits us from learning to communicate our needs more effectively or from taking responsibility for ensuring that our needs are met in other ways.

Many of us blame ourselves, perpetuating beliefs that we do not deserve to have the kind of life that we desire. We spend too much time telling ourselves that we are at fault and too little time doing the things that would make a tangible difference. Blame takes energy, it restricts our ability to see and act upon the many opportunities that are available to us. When we blame ourselves we are essentially repeating beliefs that we are not good enough and that we do not trust ourselves to be successful. Whether we blame ourselves or others, the energy of our blaming thoughts keeps us attached to our problems rather than liberating us from them.

VICTIM NO MORE!

Many of us have learned to think of ourselves as victims. We can be faced with any challenge, from the car breaking down to a misunderstanding with a friend or from stubbing a toe to a period of illness, and allow ourselves to repeat patterns of victim mentality. There is a difference between expressing appropriate feelings of sadness, disappointment or frustration when we are dealing with something challenging and repeating victim thoughts that keep us small or powerless.

When we think of ourselves as victims we often react as if we have been singled out for divine retribution; we take everything personally and carry what we perceive to be the injustices of the world on our shoulders. We say things like, 'Everyone has got it in for me,' 'Somebody up there must really hate me,' 'Life is so unfair,' 'Why does it always happen to me?' and 'Life's a bitch and then you die.' The problem with thinking like this is that it disempowers us; we rob ourselves of many of the resources or solutions that we need to handle our challenge and move beyond it. What is more, victim mentality makes us more available to people, situations and experiences that perpetuate the

If you recognize any of this in yourself it is time to make a new choice: victim no more!

GILLIAN'S STORY

Gillian was a woman in her forties who came to me for healing at the same time that she was undergoing medical treatment for breast cancer. Her cancer had been detected in its early stages and was eminently treatable, but understandably she was still quite shocked and distressed by her diagnosis. She spent her time with me coming to terms with the emotional and psychological effects of her condition and exploring ways that she could help prevent a reoccurrence of her symptoms.

When we met, I asked Gillian to talk about her past experiences and her future aspirations. I particularly wanted to find out what was happening in her life for the few years prior to her diagnosis and I needed to listen for any mental, emotional or environmental factors that could have contributed to her condition. As she talked Gillian listed a catalogue of disappointing or destructive relationships that she had had in her life, from her relationship with her parents to her relationships with her ex-husband and the boyfriends that she had lived with following the breakdown of her marriage. She even described the relationship that she had with her children as 'loving but hurtful'.

It became clear from the language that she used that Gillian viewed herself as one of life's survivors and also as one of life's victims. She talked a great deal about what 'they' did to her and how she was 'powerless in the situation'. She talked of her cancer too as if it were something that life had inflicted upon her, another trial that she had to endure, something else that she had to suffer through. While I was sympathetic to many of the challenges that she had faced in the past and to the challenge that she was presently facing, I could hear many deeply held negative beliefs that were supporting

108   her victim role and I also detected some old, unexpressed feelings of grief that were contributing to her current state of distress.

I told Gillian that to support the success of her treatments and help to prevent future illness it would benefit her to begin to think about her life in a different way. I said that if she continued to talk about herself as a victim she would continue to invite more relationships and experiences into her life that would perpetuate her victim role. We began to look at why she might have chosen her relationships and what she could learn from them. We also spent some time building a new vocabulary of thoughts and beliefs that would help her to become more powerful and effective in everything that she wished to create.

As she began to use the ideas and techniques that I suggested, the sense of grief that I was picking up from Gillian increased until one day I finally asked her the question, *'Are you grieving for someone?'* She immediately burst into tears and told me that her mother had died eight years previously and that she had never properly grieved or had a chance to say goodbye. We talked about what her mother was like when she was alive and Gillian told me that, like her, her mother had always been one of life's survivors and one of life's victims. In fact, she had lived her life so much in the victim role that she had often been unavailable to nurture and support Gillian as she was growing up, despite the fact that she loved her dearly.

Gillian made some new decisions about herself and about how she was going to live her life from that point onwards. She decided that she needed to give herself space to take care of the feelings that she had not acknowledged and addressed in the past, but that in doing so she owed it to herself and her mother to live her life differently. She decided to take some time off from her many commitments to nurture herself as she continued with her treatment, filling her life with lots of positive attention from friends, therapists and health care professionals. She also made a commitment to herself to continue talking about her relationship with her mother, first with me and then with a bereavement counsellor.

With every new choice that she made in her life Gillian asked herself, *'As a liberated, powerful, self-determining woman, what do I want to do?'* She constantly thought about how she might handle things from a victim role and how she would prefer to handle things from a position of power, taking the steps that best strengthened her new, positive view of herself. She continued to use her affirmations to support her efforts.

Gillian did respond well to her treatment and three years later was still in full health, although her life was quite different. She had created a new, loving relationship which was working well and was completely unlike the relationships she had had in the past. She and her boyfriend had made a commitment to each other which included an agreement to take plenty of time to play together, travel together and have quiet time away from their other commitments to nurture each other.

Affirmations for Exercising Your Personal Power

Here are some of the affirmations that I suggested for Gillian:

- IT IS SAFE FOR ME TO BE POWERFUL.

- IT IS SAFE FOR ME TO TAKE RESPONSIBILITY FOR MY HEALTH AND HAPPINESS.

- MY ACTIONS AND NEW CHOICES ALWAYS BRING REWARDS.

- I EASILY HARNESS THE POWER OF THE PRESENT MOMENT.

- MY IMPACT IS POSITIVE, POWERFUL AND EFFECTIVE.

- IT IS SAFE FOR ME TO LIVE IN THE PRESENT.

- MY LIFE IS ALWAYS SUCCESSFUL.

In leaving behind our victim roles, stepping into our personal power and seizing the opportunity of creating our lives anew in this present moment it is always valuable to ask, *'As a powerful, liberated person, what is the best choice that I can make at this time?'*

BEING AVAILABLE FOR SIMPLE SOLUTIONS

Healing is often an ongoing process of discovering and applying a combination of solutions. Perhaps we take care of our symptoms with some form of physical treatment which leads us on to making some attitudinal changes, which in turn facilitates some emotional release which makes us available for some treatment that is even more appropriate and effective. Gently we are able to release our symptoms, deal with their underlying cause and make sense of our experiences until we have transformed our condition or until we have found new ways to manage and transcend it. However, to heal ourselves it is also important to be available for the one simple step that could change everything easily and rapidly.

In some cases healing occurs because there is one simple solution that can be discovered and applied. We discover the appropriate treatment or make one simple but profound change in attitude and healing occurs as if by magic. We always need to remain open-minded enough to discover the simple solutions and be willing to have the courage to apply them when they are staring us in the face. For example, when we know that one particular kind of food creates a disturbance within our bodies, our emotions and our mental state then the simple solution is to eliminate that food from our diet. We just need to be willing to take that step. Here are some affirmations to use to help you to recognize and use the

Affirmations for Simple Solutions

- IT IS EASY FOR ME TO RECOGNIZE AND APPLY THE OBVIOUS SOLUTIONS.

- I AM WILLING TO ALLOW THE PROCESS OF HEALING TO BE SIMPLE AND EASY.

- I WAKE UP TO THE CHANGES THAT I NEED TO MAKE IN MY LIFE.

- I HAVE THE COURAGE TO CHANGE FOR THE BETTER.

- I HAVE THE COURAGE TO HEAL MYSELF.

- I AM WILLING TO TAKE THE NEXT AVAILABLE STEP FORWARD IN MY HEALING PROCESS.

- MY HEALING IS SIMPLE AND EASY.

- I DISCOVER THE PERFECT HEALING SOLUTIONS FOR MY NEEDS.

- I HAVE THE STRENGTH AND SUPPORT TO APPLY MY HEALING SOLUTIONS EFFECTIVELY.

Becoming available for the simple solutions requires us to let go of any beliefs that we may have learned about life being a struggle, hard work or a drama. So often we have learned from our parents, our schooling and our own life experience that the day-to-day reality of the world is a constant battle which we rarely win. When we let go of the struggle words and beliefs that we hold we discover that it does not have to be like this and we make ourselves available for the simple solutions that we need.

Many times I have experienced someone with a simple solution to his or her problems who creates the most extraordinary drama that obscures or greatly delays a safe and straightforward resolution. Perhaps we all do this to some extent; the mastery of life comes with a willingness to have things be easy and to notice when we are over-complicating or obstructing our path forward.

DISSOLVING THE BLOCKS

Many of us talk about feeling blocked or stuck. Perhaps we feel emotionally blocked and unable to express our feelings, or sometimes we think that our minds are blocked, going round and round in circles, stuck with the same old patterns of thought. At other times we perceive the blocks as being outside of ourselves. It could be the structure of our job that appears to prevent us from being more creative, or a physical condition that refuses to heal. Whatever it is, by first dissolving the block in our perception we can help ourselves to move forward in life, freeing up feelings, relationships and situations in the process.

Visualization: Dissolving the Blocks

Think for a moment about any areas of your life where you feel particularly stuck or blocked. If there are no blocks in your life then that is good, you do not need to create them for the purpose of this exercise, just celebrate and move on. However, if you do feel blocked in any area it may help you to visualize it in one of the following ways:

- Picture your block as a large wall. (Decide for yourself what it might be made of, bricks perhaps or stones or even a mass of negative thoughts.) Once you have an idea in your mind about this wall, use your imagination to see yourself getting beyond it. You could see yourself tunnelling underneath, walking calmly around the side, vaulting over it, blowing it up, knocking it down, dissolving it with a flood of water, transforming it into something soft or beautiful that is easy to pass through, putting in a gate and walking through, bathing it in healing light that dissolves it completely – the choices are endless, just use the images that make the most sense to you.

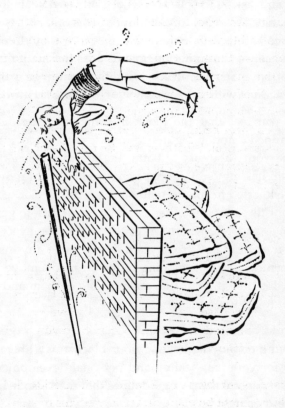

- Alternatively, picture your block as a fire-breathing dragon angrily belching flame. Imagine yourself showering this dragon with love and acceptance, standing your ground and bathing this creature with healing light to soothe or pacify it. Picture your dragon growing smaller and becoming calmer, transforming into a happy creature that assumes a manageable size and a pleasing appearance. Make friends with your dragon now that you have tamed it and ask it to tell you what you need to help you to change. Listen for any thoughts, ideas or instincts that you have and make a note of them, even if they do not make any sense to you at this time. It does not matter if you do not have any particular insights; just imagine that your dragon is willing to assist you in moving forward.

- If you feel that the block is somewhere inside you as trapped emotion, tightened muscles or areas of stress, just use your thoughts to bathe the appropriate part of you with healing light. Perhaps envision the light moving into the knotted feeling in your stomach or the blocked area of your throat or any other area that feels stuck to gently dissolve and release any trapped energy. See every part of you as fluid and free. Again, if you have any insights or practical ideas concerning how you might move forward at this time in your life, make a note of them and remember to act upon them.

Dissolving or moving beyond your blocks may liberate some energy for your self-healing and personal development. Here are some general ideas or guidelines that may also help you to raise your energy.

When we are sick or when we feel stuck in a job or a relationship that is unhealthy for us we sometimes stop ourselves from changing the situation because we do not believe that we have the energy to do so. We say that we are too tired, too busy, too sick or too old to be able to summon up the necessary energy. Sometimes we just feel too trapped to be able to galvanize ourselves and move forward.

We all have much more energy than we often credit ourselves with, it is just that in most cases we have not learned to unleash, harness and use the power that we were born with. Our energy gets tied up in:

Negative Thinking:
Negative thoughts are heavy and slow. They deplete us physically and emotionally while trapping our energy in unused potential or frustrated creative expression.

Unexpressed Emotion:
Emotions themselves are energy, so unexpressed emotions amount to a great deal of trapped healing potential. In addition, it takes a great deal more energy to suppress our feelings and desires than it does to express them. Just consider this for a moment: for every area of sadness, anger, joy, passion and excitement that you have not learned to acknowledge or express healthily, you are denying yourself all of that energy *and* using up a great deal more keeping these emotions under wraps.

Joyless Activities:
Most of us at some time or another tie up our energy in joyless activities. Have you noticed that some things that you do give you energy and others seem to take it or drain it away? Even

tasks that leave us physically tired can be energizing; because we enjoy them they leave us feeling fulfilled and joyful. Often after a good sleep we will feel refreshed, renewed and ready to start again.

In contrast, there are the joyless activities that we fill our lives with. These are the things that we do because we feel that we *ought* to do them rather than because we want to. Often it is because somebody else wants us to do them or because when we were children our parents told us that we *ought* to do them. When we do not do what we love, or do not learn to love what we do, our energy levels decrease.

Here is a checklist for releasing and creating energy:

A Checklist for Releasing and Creating Energy

- Create something new. Express your creativity in some way – write a poem, bake a pasta dish, draw a picture, create a new computer programme, write a letter, arrange some flowers; find some way to express your creativity, no matter how small it may seem.

- Take a positive risk. Join a class, go to a personal development course, do something new, make a new friend, speak to somebody new at work, make a telephone call that you have been putting off, learn a new skill, dress in a different way, plan a holiday or a fun day out; remember to stretch out the boundaries at your own pace.

- Be honest with someone. Ask for what you want, talk about how you feel, say *'I love you'*, give praise and encouragement, say *'no'* when you mean no and *'yes'* when you mean yes, calmly and clearly asserting your needs; take simple, gentle steps as you do this and praise yourself for your successes.

- Be honest with yourself. Acknowledge your true feelings, be honest about your dreams, ambitions or desires, recognize some areas of your resistance to change or recognize behaviour that is unhealthy for you in some way. Remember to do all of this without judging or criticizing yourself.

- Forgive someone. Acknowledge and then let go of your resentments. Acknowledge and then let go of vengeful thoughts. Breathe into the feelings of sadness or anger, hurt or disappointment that you have around another person in your life and then declare to yourself, *'I am willing to forgive, I am willing to let go of the past and prepare myself for better experiences.'*

- Forgive yourself. Acknowledge and let go of your feelings of guilt. Stop punishing yourself for the things that you did or did not do in the past. Refuse to criticize yourself for anything that cannot now be changed. Make positive, loving changes in how you handle similar situations now. Declare to yourself, '*I am willing to forgive myself, I am willing to let go of the past and release myself into joy.*'

- Change the thought. Every time you think '*I never have any energy*' then you rob yourself of energy; every time you say '*It is such hard work*' then you do not allow for the possibility that it can get easier. Whenever there is a lack of energy, motivation or drive then there is usually a thought, belief or expectation that needs to be changed. Start acknowledging and appreciating the energy that you have got rather than always focusing on your fatigue and, bit by bit, your energy level will improve.

- Change your diet. Heavy, processed foods take energy to digest without giving much in return. Whole foods, fresh fruit, fresh vegetables, organically produced foods and foods that are lovingly prepared are generally easier to digest, and provide energy.

    There is no such thing as the ideal diet for everyone, one person's healing diet could be completely inappropriate for somebody else.

- Change your habits. If you smoke, smoke a little less. If you drink alcohol, drink a little less. Substances like sugar, salt or the caffeine in your coffee and tea may give you an initial energy buzz but are soon energy depleting. Of course it would be better not to smoke at all and to drink only a little alcohol, but giving up any substance entirely needs to be done at your own pace. A sensible reduction will certainly help your energy levels.

- Do something active. Go to an exercise class, take the dog for a walk, get up from your seat and stretch; if you are disabled or sick then stretch or exercise gently in the best way you can, taking appropriate advice from a doctor, a physiotherapist or a complementary health practitioner.

- Replace a joyless activity with a joyful one. Little by little, let go of the activities that do not energize you or bring you joy. If, for example, you watch three hours of television a day out of habit but do not actively enjoy it, cut down on your viewing time a little and replace it with other activities that you enjoy more. What are the things that you do out of habit or because you feel you ought to? One by one replace them with something healthier and happier.

The ideas above are just a starting point for your own imaginative thoughts and actions. Doing just one thing can change your energy level and help to raise your motivation and drive in other areas of your life. If your energy is stuck or lacking then there is always something that you can do, no matter how small, to make a difference.

YOUR SPIRITUAL JOURNEY

A SPIRITUAL PERSPECTIVE

I believe that we are more than just a body, a collection of emotions and a series of thoughts. The more that I learn about the nature of self-healing, the more I am convinced that the most profound transformation occurs when we are willing to acknowledge that there is a greater aspect of ourselves.

Imagine that there is a part of you that sees the bigger picture of your life and is able to direct you towards your highest joy. This part of you is quite different from your conscious mind, which appears to be directing everything during your waking hours. This part of you is able to see beyond the mental limitations that you place upon yourself and, if you allow it to, will help you to stay healthy and happy.

It is not important whether we have a firm spiritual belief that this is the part of ourselves connected to God, or instead take a less spiritually-based view of life and see this greater aspect of ourselves as an area of our minds that we have yet to learn more about; either way we can learn to work with our greater awareness to help us heal ourselves.

Some people call it the higher self, the higher mind or the

god-self. Others may describe it as their over-soul, greater consciousness or higher wisdom. It really does not matter what we call it, how it fits into our religious or spiritual philosophy or even if we hold a firm belief that it exists – just being willing to entertain the possibility that there is a wise spiritual being inside each of us can bring dramatic changes.

Most of my work has been concerned with helping to prolong and enhance life, but there have been many times when I have supported people who are dealing with a serious illness or, in some cases, facing death. A long time ago I dispensed with many of my judgements about what healing is 'supposed to' look like. For some of us, healing occurs when our symptoms disappear and their underlying causes dissolve; for others, healing is concerned with reaching a greater understanding of themselves and finding grace and dignity as they come to terms with their illness or their death. Whatever our path, our greater awareness can help us to make sense of what is happening to us and put our lives into perspective.

When I am helping people to heal themselves, I often feel as if I am helping them to negotiate between their conscious mind and their greater awareness, encouraging them to integrate their higher wisdom more effectively into their daily lives so that it may direct their healing process. This part of them is often the part that is offering the healing solutions and, if listened to, will provide information that will guide them towards their greatest potential.

THE SPIRITUAL PURPOSE OF ILLNESS

Some of us create illness or problems as a way of directing ourselves towards our greatest joy. It may not always feel like this at moments when we are in pain or dealing with symptoms that restrict our mobility and impede our lives, but I have seen so many people grow through their illnesses, becoming more aware of themselves, more mature and often more spiritually focused. It helps when we can begin to view everything that happens to us as an opportunity rather than as a disaster.

I do not believe that illness is an essential part of our growth and development; it is just one way that we express and resolve our inner conflicts and move ourselves towards our higher potential. Often we can prevent illness and accelerate healing by being willing to find other ways to grow and integrate our spiritual lessons. Whether we are currently dealing with, or wish to prevent an illness, an ongoing condition or a challenging series of problems, it is important to seize the spiritual opportunity of each new moment. You can begin by asking yourself the question, *'How can I best move beyond my old limitations to become all that I was created to be?'*

Exercise: The Message of Illness

Find somewhere quiet and comfortable to sit and have a pen and paper to hand. Start by sitting with your body open and relaxed. Close your eyes and breathe deeply, just as you would if you were beginning a visualization. In your mind, ask for help in locating and releasing the underlying cause of any illness or ailments that you are currently dealing with. Ask too for new ways to deal with any long-term conditions or recurring problems, and declare that you are available for transformational changes of attitude. When you feel centred and ready, open your eyes and write your instinctive answers to the following questions:

'What have my problems or illness got to teach me at this time?'

'What do I need to learn that will aid my happiness and well-being?'

'What do I need to do to release my condition or problems and move on?'

Do your best not to judge or limit the answers that you receive, even if they do not make sense to you at this time. Do not worry if you do not receive any insights immediately, it is often enough to ask the right questions for a process of healing to be set in motion. Also, allowing yourself to answer instinctively can take practice. Make sure that you act upon any relevant ideas, and complete the process by affirming:

- I AM WILLING TO FOLLOW MY UNIQUE SPIRITUAL PATH.

- I AM AVAILABLE FOR MY HIGHEST GOOD.

- I AM ALWAYS GUIDED TOWARDS HEALTH AND JOY.

Repeat this exercise regularly, staying open to new insights and new changes of attitude that could make a difference to your ongoing process of self-healing.

CREATING A LIFE WITH PURPOSE

I have discovered that the healthiest people are often those who create for themselves a life of meaning and purpose. If we have a vision of what we wish to create, things that we want to do and an opportunity to contribute something of ourselves to the world around us, then we tend to be supported in health, happiness and spiritual growth. Older people who stay healthy and animated long after they have passed retirement age are often those who actively seek new things to learn and new ways to contribute to others.

We sometimes expect life to provide us with a purpose or meaning and we wait for other people to take the initiative of inviting us to participate in our own personal development. The truth is that we are always invited to take part in the adventure of life, but it is up to us to seize that opportunity. If your life does not appear to have a meaning, create one for yourself. If you are lacking direction then take some time to listen to your underlying purpose. The clues are always there. What motivates you? What inspires you? What do you desire? What engages your interest? The things that we feel passionate about act as the road signs for our healing journey. They tell us where we need to go to fulfil our spiritual purpose.

SEEING THE BIGGER PICTURE

We are usually so immersed in the day-to-day dramas of our lives that we do not see the bigger picture. We rush around doing our best to fulfil all of our commitments, take care of the people that we love, stay financially solvent and deal with our physical or emotional challenges, and in doing so we forget that there may be a greater purpose to our lives. We forget to look at our overall direction, neglecting to draw a distinction between the things that we do out of habit, guilt or a lack of imagination and the things that we do because they actively move our lives forward.

Sometimes we emerge from our routines and dramas to see our lives with greater clarity. We are suddenly able to make sense of our experiences and see the obvious solutions to the challenges we are facing. At these times of clarity we may gain great insight into the meaning and purpose of everything that is happening to us; we may even develop a sense of Divine inspiration. An example is when we suddenly understand in our hearts something that we have understood intellectually

for some time and have not been able to apply. Grasping the feeling of something rather than just the idea can make a transformational difference to us.

Some illnesses provide us with a 'bridge' to the bigger picture of our lives. At times we create illnesses as a way of diverting ourselves from a path we are taking that no longer serves us and on to a new one that will allow us to grow. At other times we use them to slow ourselves down so that we can allow space for our dreams, desires and inner feelings to direct us beyond our old limiting beliefs.

MIKE'S STORY

Mike came to me when he was suffering with chronic fatigue syndrome (ME). He had always been an active person and found the limitations of his condition unbearably frustrating and uncomfortable. He felt impotent and unable to make any headway in his life.

Before becoming sick, Mike had been a high-powered executive in a company that manufactured stationery and office furnishings. For a long time he had been satisfied with his job, but about four years previously he had inexplicably reached a point where he no longer felt motivated and inspired by the challenges that his work offered him.

Desperate to regain his motivation, Mike pushed himself harder and harder at work in the hope that he would develop some new areas of business that would inspire him to carry on. After all, he was in a good, safe position that was well paid and reasonably creative; it did not occur to him that he might need to be doing something completely different with his life. The less motivated and inspired that he felt, the more that he pushed himself on, reminding himself of what his father had always told him: 'Life is 10 per cent inspiration and 90 per cent perspiration.'

Mike began to experience sudden losses of energy and co-ordination. At moments he was unable to think clearly and for the first time in his career he was forced to take time off work. Whenever his energy and clarity returned he would feel buoyant, conveniently forgetting how ill he had been, and he would drive himself even harder to catch up with his workload. He continued like this for nearly three years, steadily getter sicker and needing to take longer periods off work, until finally his energy seemed to escape him completely and he was forced to resign.

When Mike first came to see me for hands-on healing he was still quite ill. He would have occasional days when his symptoms would disappear dramatically and he would confidently begin to do more. However, a day of greater energy and activity was usually followed by several days of exhaustion, and he often felt as if he were back at square one. What struck me about Mike was how guilty he felt about being sick and how harshly he judged himself for failing to get better and return to work. I also realized how much Mike had valued himself as a dependable and efficient executive and how little he valued himself now that he was unable to fulfil that role.

I encouraged Mike to let go of his harsh judgements and I told him that he would emerge from his condition when he stopped fighting and surrendered to it fully. I also encouraged him to love and value himself regardless of what he was or was not able to do. One morning soon afterwards, Mike woke up with a sudden realization of his situation. It was still very early but he was instantly wide awake.

Mike felt very clear-headed and there was an extraordinary feeling of warmth that spread from his toes upwards through every part of his body. He felt very peaceful and he had a powerful understanding of how he had created his illness, what he had done to himself in forcing himself to continue working beyond his endurance and how he needed to let go and trust the process of his life. After a while, he became drowsy again and fell into a deep, peaceful sleep that was unlike anything that he had experienced since he was a child.

After that, Mike allowed himself to surrender to his condition and even permitted himself to enjoy the peace and stillness of his life. He reflected upon how he had enjoyed many aspects of his job but he realized that he had never really wanted a high-powered position, he had just allowed himself to be promoted upwards because he felt that he *ought* to do the sensible, dependable thing – which for him meant working his way up the career ladder just as his father had done.

Mike's energy levels started to return quite dramatically, but he chose to continue to take things gently. When he was ready he began to take courses in meditation and yoga; as he meditated he often experienced the warm, peaceful feeling that he had felt in his body on the morning that he became more aware of himself.

When Mike did return to work he started off with part-time jobs and then graduated to taking a responsible, non-executive position that allowed him to be quite creative while leaving him enough time and energy to do the other things he enjoyed.

Mike continued his meditation practice and began to study

comparative religions, something that he had always wanted to do. He also made sure he could always take the occasional day out to do absolutely nothing except contemplate his navel if he so desired. Mike learned to value himself for who he was, not what he did for a living, and he became much happier than he had ever been. He told me that his most important step forward had been allowing himself to be a reflective person and not just an active one.

TAKING YOUR NEXT STEPS FORWARD

Sometimes we are so scared of taking the next step forward and moving out into the unknown that we procrastinate and resist making new choices or decisions. We may even resist using our chosen affirmations because we are scared of affirming for the wrong thing. We need to develop trust in ourselves and in the process of life so that we can step beyond our old limitations with an open mind and heart. Here are some affirmations to help:

Need or Challenge:

- *'I am scared of affirming for the wrong thing; I know that my mind is powerful and I am frightened that I will create something that I cannot handle.'*

Affirmations:

- I AM ENOUGH.

- I TRUST MYSELF.

- I CREATE ONLY LOVING, JOYOUS AND HARMONIOUS EXPERIENCES IN MY LIFE.

- MY AFFIRMATIONS ARE ALWAYS ALIGNED TO MY HIGHEST JOY.

Need or Challenge:

- *'I know what it is that I need to be doing but I am scared of taking that first step.'*

Affirmations:

- IT IS EASY FOR ME TO TAKE THE NEXT STEP FORWARD.

- I EASILY ACT UPON MY KNOWLEDGE AND INSIGHTS.

- I AM ALWAYS SUPPORTED IN TAKING ACTION THAT IS IN LINE WITH MY HIGHEST GOOD.

Sometimes we resist taking the next steps forward because we cannot imagine what life would be like be without our illness or the problems that we are currently facing. If, in contrast, we actively engage our imagination to build a picture and a feeling of our healthy, happy, future self, we fuel our inspiration and strengthen our ability to create our lives in the way that we choose.

Visualization: Taking the Next Steps

Find somewhere quiet and comfortable to sit, unplug the telephone and make sure that you are not going to be disturbed. Sit with your back supported, your body open and relaxed with your arms and legs uncrossed. If you prefer you can lie down for this, but again make sure that you keep your body open rather than curled up.

Breathe long, slow, deep breaths. When you have settled, imagine that you are now free of your current problems and challenges. Picture yourself as healthy, whole and complete, with relationships that are harmonious and wonderful new opportunities continually opening up for you. Imagine that you are magnetic to love and approval, attracting positive, loving attention whenever you need it. See yourself smiling and happy, able to enjoy the adventure of life, safe and protected wherever you go.

In your mind's eye, develop a picture of what you might do to create this state of affairs. What steps would you take in your life right now to facilitate your health and happiness? Do you need to rest or slow down? Do you need to seek help? Do you need to explore new treatments or gain more information about the treatments that are available to you? What do you need to do for your spiritual growth and personal development at this time?

Visualize yourself easily taking the steps that you need to create the healing that you desire. Imagine that you have a special talent for self-healing and positive transformation.

When you complete this exercise, write down or record any insights that you had during it, and remember to take those valuable steps forward.

BLESS WITH LOVE AND MOVE ON

Taking the next steps in our lives always requires us to bless with love the experiences, relationships and problems that we are leaving behind and move on. Our impulse to learn and to grow is always moving us forward on our spiritual path; we are frequently required to let go of what is familiar to us in order to grasp the opportunity of new health, new life and new awareness. We tend to have a fear of the unknown and we may have a desire to stay with what we already know; however, to embrace the ongoing adventure of healing we all need to take the risk of thinking, acting and responding to life in new ways.

INDEX

About nine years ago I spent an intensive few months participating in personal development courses, putting my past into perspective, moving beyond my limiting expectations and planning for the life that I wanted to create. It was a fascinating time, filled with interesting people to learn from, some loving and supportive and some quite the opposite, but all teaching me by their example about the new choices that I needed to make for myself.

When my life started to move on and some of the things that I had planned for began to happen – such as a wonderful new relationship, a new place to live and some new opportunities to use my talents – I was initially resistant, wanting to hold on to what was familiar. My feelings came to a head at the end of the penultimate session of a support group that I had been attending. I felt sad to be leaving some members of the group and angry with others because of things that had happened between us. On returning to my home, the anger was the feeling that was most present and I decided to write down some of my thoughts and feelings so that I could make sense of them.

When I picked up a pen and paper to write, a voice inside stopped me and I had a strong impulse to meditate instead. I sat comfortably, began to breathe deeply and allowed myself to settle into a state of relaxation. As I did so, the thought sprang into my mind, *'It is safe for me to trust and let go; it is safe for me to move on.'* With these words going around in my head I became very peaceful. After a while, I fell asleep.

When I awoke I had an immediate impulse to write; as I picked up my pen I heard music in my head. Although I was hardly aware of what I was doing, within a short time I had written the words to a song. I would like to share them with you here.

Golden Light – I Forgive

There's a golden light around me to take away my fears,
there's a golden love surrounds me as I wipe away the
    tears,
my life has been so busy, my anger been so strong,
all the people that surround me that I once felt did me
    wrong,
but I forgive and I grow strong, I forgive and move
    along.

There's a light shines through that doorway that calls me
    to step through,
and the sun shows through the trees that live for me in
    pastures new,
sometimes I feel bitter but I shed it like a skin,
sometimes I feel so helpless but I let my passion win,
and I forgive and I grow strong, I forgive and move
    along.

Shed my body, find a new one,
shed my pain and find some joy,
shed all the things that hurt me when I was a little boy,
and finally I bathe myself in pools of deepest blue,
and finally surrender to the beauty that is you,

and I believe in you and me, I believe that I am free.

I forgive and I grow strong, I forgive and move along,
move along and shed my skin and I let my passion win,
I forgive and I grow strong, I forgive...
and now I'm gone...